CHILDREN OF POVERTY

STUDIES ON THE EFFECTS
OF SINGLE PARENTHOOD,
THE FEMINIZATION OF POVERTY,
AND HOMELESSNESS

edited by

STUART BRUCHEY
UNIVERSITY OF MAINE

A GARLAND SERIES

NO PLACE ELSE TO GO

HOMELESS MOTHERS AND THEIR CHILDREN LIVING IN URBAN SHELTERS

SHARON R. LIFF

GARLAND PUBLISHING, INC.
NEW YORK & LONDON / 1996

3-12-99

Library of Congress Cataloging-in-Publication Data

Liff, Sharon R..
    No place else to go : homeless mothers and their children
living in urban shelters / Sharon R. Liff.
        p.   cm. — (Children of poverty)
    Includes bibliographical references and index.
    ISBN 0-8153-2436-7 (alk. paper)
    1. Shelters for the homeless—New York (N.Y.) 2. Homeless
women—Services for—New York (N.Y.) 3. Homeless children—
Services for—New York (N.Y.) 4. Single mothers—New York
(N.Y.)—Social conditions. 5. Poor women—New York (N.Y.)
6. Feminist theory. I. Title. II. Series.
HV4506.N6L53 1996
363.5'8—dc20   95-53203

Printed on acid-free, 250-year-life paper
Manufactured in the United States of America

To my children, Joshua Franklin and Danielle Lily

Contents

viii

ACKNOWLEDGMENTS

I would like to thank the many people who helped me with this project which started out as my doctoral dissertation at New York University and eventually became this book. First, I would like to express gratitude to my committee chairperson, Iris Fodor, who read many drafts of the manuscript and provided ideas, support and structure. I also want to thank Margot Ely who gave so generously of her time and supported all my efforts. She introduced me to the methodology and taught me much of what I know about it.

And thanks also to Sandy Barbo, a fellow researcher who met with me since the beginning of the project and provided feedback about the data and analysis.

A special thank you to the mothers and children who willingly shared their pain and hardship as well as their hopes, dreams, and fears.

I gratefully acknowledge the Henry A. Murray Research Center of Radcliffe College for the dissertation award which helped to support the project.

Finally, I would like to thank my husband, Jerome, who helped with editing and typing. His assistance as well as encouragement were invaluable. I would also like to thank my parents and sister for their support.

No Place Else to Go

I

Introduction

There has been a marked increase in the number of homeless families in the United States since 1982 (Committee on Government Operations, 1986). Families have become a significant part of the homeless population particularly in the last decade (Bassuk, 1993; Rossi, 1994; Weinreb and Rossi, 1995). In New York City, 2,416 families were placed in shelters or welfare hotels by December 1983 and this number rose to 5,083 by September 1988 (Citizen's Committee for Children of New York, 1988). Although the number has decreased somewhat since then it remains substantial. In January 1991, 3,967 homeless families lived in shelters in New York City (Morgan, 1991). While the media have been quick to illuminate the plight of children and families housed in shelters or hotels because of lack of more adequate housing, researchers have not followed suit. Little formal research has been conducted about the families with children who are housed in shelters or hotels, sometimes for many years.

Several recent studies have illuminated the negative effects of homelessness on children (Bassuk and Rubin, 1987; Masten, Miliotis, Graham-Bermann, Ramirez and Neeman, 1993; Rescorla, Parker and Stolky, 1991). One of the few investigators (Bassuk and Rubin, 1987) who assessed the characteristics of homeless children living in a shelter found that they were developmentally delayed, depressed, anxious and had difficulty learning. Further, Bassuk and Rubin (1987) estimated that at least fifty percent of these children needed to be referred for psychiatric evaluation. Homeless mothers have also been found to exhibit high levels of depression (Rog, McCombs-Thornton, Gilbert-Mongelli, Brito and Halupka, 1995). Clearly, these families are living with multiple stressors that have been correlated with the development of emotional disturbance (Rutter, 1981). Prevalent stressors include trauma such as witnessing fire or violence, multiple moves, poverty and overcrowded living conditions (Citizens Committee for Children of New York, 1988; Community Service Society of New York, 1984).

Prolonged or extreme stress has frequently been associated with emotional and physical symptomatology. For example, depression and anxiety have been linked to stressful life events (American Psychiatric Association, 1987). Post-traumatic stress has recently been designated as a specific disorder that frequently occurs following exposure to unusual and extreme events (American Psychiatric Association, 1987). Homelessness has been viewed as a form of psychological trauma (Goodman, Saxe & Harvey, 1991). However, not everyone exposed to similar events develops emotional symptoms to the same degree or at all.

Coping is a concept that has been developed as a way to view varying responses to stressful life events. Researchers have begun to devote more attention to the way children, adults, and families cope with a variety of stressful events (Lazarus & Folkman, 1984; McCubbin & Figley, 1983; Murphy & Moriarty, 1976). They have identified many factors that appear to make a difference in how people cope and adapt.

The view of coping that guides this study is that posed by Lazarus and Folkman (1984) who define coping as "constantly changing cognitive and behavioral efforts to manage specific external and/or internal demands that are appraised as taxing or exceeding the resources of the person"(p. 141). Coping strategies allow people to avoid feelings of distress and maintain positive self-esteem (Menaghan, 1983).

This study focuses on homelessness as a stressful life event. The impact of homelessness on families has not been well documented. Most of the research has been done by advocacy groups (Citizen's Committee for Children of New York, 1988; 1984; Coalition for the Homeless, 1984; Simpson and Kilduff, 1984) who have reported on the extremely negative process and conditions faced by families once they become homeless. While extremely important in calling attention to the situation, the reports have done little to describe how these families manage to cope and how some, in time, successfully manage to improve their situation.

In response to the lack of adequate research on homeless families and children (Bassuk & Rubin, 1987), this study describes how such families experience and cope with homelessness. For the purposes of this study homeless families are considered to be those living in a temporary shelter after having lost a former permanent residence. Families included in this study consist of a female head of household and her school age children. Female headed households were chosen because they represent the largest group of homeless families (Citizen's Committee for Children of New York, 1988). Qualitative interview methodology was used as it was particularly compatible with the aims of this study.

It is hoped that the present study will contribute to the understanding of the growing number of mothers and children who experience homelessness and provide directions for further inquiry that can result in useful insights for professionals working with these families. It seems likely that we can learn how best to help these families from those who have already experienced homelessness.

As the data were collected and analyzed the research questions were developed and refined. In qualitative research this is often the case as it is important not to pre-impose categories on the data. The following final research questions guided the study and provided a focus and framework.

1. How did these families become homeless?
2. How did these mothers and children experience the shelter system both past and present?
3. What impact do they report their experiences in the shelter system have had on various aspects of their lives?
   a. emotional and physical well being
   b. relationships
   c. schooling for children
4. How have these mothers and children utilized social supports?
5. What coping strategies have they used?

II

Review of the Literature

Despite the seriousness of the issue, there is a paucity of research on mothers and children who live in temporary shelters. This chapter summarizes the existing literature on homeless families and reviews the literature on stress and coping that informs this study.

HOMELESS FAMILIES

Prior to 1982, the homeless population was predominantly single men and women, many of whom suffered from alcoholism or chronic mental illness (Sullivan & Damrosch, 1987). Homelessness was not considered a major problem for families (Coalition for the Homeless, 1984). The picture has changed dramatically. Families are now considered to be the fastest growing subgroup within the homeless population (Bassuk, 1993). The number of homeless families rose from 2,416 in December 1983 (Citizens Committee for Children of New York, 1988) to approximately 3,967 as of January 1991 (Morgan, 1991). As a rough estimate, assuming that each family has two children the approximate number of homeless children would be 7,934. A number which is likely to be much higher since many families have more than two children. In addition to families already placed in city shelters, there are many more poised on the brink of homelessness. This section offers a preliminary description of these homeless families.

Intrafamilial Factors

While some researchers have described homeless mothers living in shelters as higher functioning than other members of the homeless population due to lower rates of substance abuse and psychiatric disorder (Weitzman, Knickman and Shinn, 1992), many researchers describe the population residing in shelters as multi-problem families. For example, Bassuk (1986) interviewed homeless mothers and children placed in six homeless shelters and two battered women's shelters and found that factors such as poverty, deprivation and violence all added to the experience of homelessness. In another study, Bassuk (1987) interviewed mothers and children in eight shelters. She found multiple problems such as chaotic developmental histories, long-term patterns of residential instability, few or no supportive relationships, family violence, poor work histories and minimal involvement with social service agencies.

Substance abuse is also a serious problem among homeless mothers (Weinrab and Bassuk,1990). Dail (1990) found that 25% of homeless mothers living in shelters admitted to alcohol or drug abuse. Rog, McCombs-Thornton, Gilbert-Mangelli, Brito and Halupka (1995) found that 74% of their sample reported past drug use while 12% admitted to drug use in the past twelve months. They also found that 29% abused alcohol. Weinreb, Brown and Berson (1995) in a study of homeless pregnant women found that one fifth of their population admitted to past or present substance abuse. The prevalence of domestic violence is reported as high in homeless mothers as well (Bassuk and Rosenberg, 1988; D'Ercole and Struening, 1990; Goodman, 1991; Wood et al., 1990; Browne, 1993; Rog et al., 1995). Weinreb, Browne and Berson (1995) found that 62% of the homeless pregnant women in their study were victims of physical abuse at some point in their lives.

Homeless children frequently exhibit developmental delays, learning difficulties, depression and anxiety (Bassuk & Rubin, 1987; Bassuk, 1987; 1986). In one study of children living in 14 family shelters (Bassuk & Rubin, 1987) half had symptoms severe enough to merit referral for psychiatric evaluation.

Homeless children frequently change schools and may spend much time out of school. Eddowes and Hranitz (1989) described the educational problems of homeless children. Gewirtzman and Fodor (1987) discussed the psychological impact of rootlessness on homeless children in school and how this engenders fear and frustration. Horowitz, Springer and Kose (1988) compared characteristics of children living in welfare hotels to children in a drop-out prevention program living in apartments. They found that children who lived in the hotels were isolated from their peers and that parents were unlikely to communicate with the school regarding their child.

Socioeconomic Factors

For many women and children in the United States, poverty is a fact of life. In 1982, 49.3 percent of all female-headed households with children lived below the poverty line (United States Bureau of the Census). Many children grow up in conditions of poverty. In 1985, 25 percent of all children living in New York State were living in poverty (New York State Council on Children and Families, 1988).

Low-income public assistance recipients comprise the majority (83%) of homeless families (HRA, 1986). In addition, most of these families consist of single mothers and their children. It is not surprising that mothers and children make up a large proportion of homeless families as poverty puts them at high risk for such an event.

Poverty and single parent status have been associated with increased risk for stressful life events (Makosky, 1982; Lindblad-Goldberg et al. 1988; McCloyd, 1990) and depression (Goldman & Ravid, 1980; Belle & Dill, 1982) in women. Other studies have found that low income, black, female single parents are faced with many sources of chronic stress that can effect their mental health and well being (Brown & Harris, 1978; Dohrenwend, 1973b; McLanahan, 1983; Peters & Massey, 1983).

In children, low income has been associated with health problems such as low birth weight, infections, anemia, and lead poisoning as well as psychological and psychosomatic problems (Egbuonu & Starfield, 1982). Economic hardship has been found to diminish the capacity for consistent and involved parenting and to adversely affect children's social and emotional functioning (McCloyd, 1990). Several longitudinal studies point to low income as a risk factor in children (Werner & Smith, 1982; Werner, 1988; Felsman & Vaillant, 1988). However, these studies have found that many children are able to cope with poverty successfully and that low income alone is not necessarily a cause of emotional difficulties.

Other researchers directly dispute reliance on socioeconomic factors as a measure of life stress (Luthar & Zigler, 1991). They argue that an individual's socioeconomic status provides no information on the process through which this status might affect the way they experience stress. In addition, studies have shown that many economically deprived children are able to adjust to this life circumstance and appear to be no different from their more advantaged peers (Garmezy, 1981; Garmezy & Nuechterlein, 1972).

Sociocultural Factors

In 1982, 59 percent of blacks and 37 percent of Hispanics living in poverty were headed by females (United States Bureau of the Census). In 1979, 45 percent of Hispanic children and 38 percent of black children were living in poverty. The majority (95%) of homeless families in New York City shelters are either black or Hispanic (HRA, 1986). This is true in other parts of the country as well. In a large scale study of homeless families in California researchers found that 61% were African American or Hispanic (Stanford Center for the Study of Families, Children and Youth, 1991). Sweeping generalizations about black or Hispanic families are not particularly useful. Still, certain common elements do exist within ethnic groups and it is important to consider these sociocultural factors. These factors, particularly as they are reflected in coping strategies and familial relationships, may have a significant effect on the way families experience homelessness.

Hispanic families. The extended family is very important in Hispanic culture and during stressful experiences families typically turn to relatives for assistance. There is a strong cultural expectation that family members will feel obligated to provide necessary assistance during a crisis (Garcia-Preto, 1982). Since Hispanics tend to rely so heavily on the family for help, they turn to social services only after exhausting all other resources (Badillo-Ghali, 1977). This pattern helps to explain the finding that many homeless families spend time staying with relatives before entering the shelter system.

In particular, Puerto Rican families tend to move back and forth between the island and the mainland which is often disruptive to family life. This migration is made particularly easy because no special papers are required. "This phenomenon reinforces many links to the island, although it also reflects repeated ruptures and renewal of ties, dismantling and reconstruction of familial and communal networks in old and new settings" (Rodriguez et al., 1980, p.2). This frequent migration would add to the stress of homeless families who had recently arrived from Puerto Rico.

Black families. Black families also rely heavily on family or others to cope with the stress of daily life (Moore Hines and Boyd-Franklin, 1982). Stack (1975) found that the black families she studied had "co-residence, kinship based exchange networks linking multiple domestic units, elastic household boundaries, and lifelong bonds to three generational households." Black families are most likely to turn to their family, friends and clergy members in times of crisis. They are reluctant to rely on mental health services and tend to do so only when other sources of help have been exhausted.

STRESS

The Stress of Losing One's Home

A recent study of homeless families (Citizens' Committee for Children of New York, 1988) found that families enter the shelter system for a variety of reasons. The most common reason was being forced to leave overcrowded, doubled up living situations where they resided with family or friends. The second most common reason cited was eviction for one of several reasons including not paying rent, sublet termination or a building conversion. Less frequent reasons included fire, vacate orders because of unsafe housing, battering or abuse by spouse, harassment by landlord, and dangerous living conditions due to criminal activity in the building. Another study of families living in a welfare hotel (Community Service Society of New York, 1984) found reasons for homelessness were, in descending order, eviction, fire, vacate orders, overcrowding, and an abusive spouse. Seltser and Miller (1992) found precipitating causes of homelessness in their Los Angeles study to be inability to pay rent, ending a relationship with someone they had been living with, eviction or inability to work due to illness or injury.

The Stress of Finding Shelter

The stress of being homeless is exacerbated by the process of finding temporary shelter. Initially, many families turn to relatives or friends for temporary shelter (Citizens' Committee for Children of New York, 1988). They may move several times, since long stays in any household may be difficult due to overcrowded conditions.

Throughout the country families are placed in shelters when they become homeless,. The number of shelters that house families has increased dramatically in response to the growing population. The US. Department of Housing and Urban Development found that the numbers of such shelters in the United States increased from 1,900 in 1984 to over 5,000 in 1989 (US. Department of Housing and Urban Development, 1984,1989). Shelters vary considerably in the amount of comfort, support and privacy they provide families (Weinreb and Rossi, 1995). In general, in New York City families turn to the city shelter system after they have exhausted all other resources. The process begins when the family goes to the welfare center to request shelter. If that center is unable to find shelter during business hours, the family must turn to the twenty-four hour Emergency Assistance Units (EAU's) operated by the city. Often the EAU is unable to find the family shelter immediately and families may spend long hours or overnight in the EAU office without shelter (Coalition for the Homeless, 1984).

The city provides temporary shelter for homeless families in three types of facilities: congregate barracks style shelters (Tier I), privately owned welfare hotels, and shelters run by nonprofit organizations (Tier II). Families are typically moved around many times once they enter the shelter system.

Congregate shelters. Initial placement is usually in a barracks style or congregate shelter where all people sleep in a large open room. The city created these facilities to provide families with temporary emergency shelter. Technically, placement in a barracks shelter is supposed to last no longer than 21 days. However, because so many families need placement, the city is often unable to find families long-term placement in the allotted 21 days. Frequently, families spend much longer in the barracks shelters with some spending as long as one year (Citizens' Committee for Children of New York, 1988).

The barracks shelters are difficult places for families with children (Citizen's Committee for Children of New York, 1988). For these families the stress of their recent homelessness is exacerbated by the congregate shelter environment. Because there are no private spaces, children may be exposed to the inappropriate behavior of other shelter residents and are placed at risk for many communicable diseases. Children are often unable to sleep because the shelters are noisy throughout the night. No provisions are provided for a quiet place for children to do their homework and recreational facilities are frequently lacking (Citizen's Committee for Children of New York, 1988).

Welfare hotels. From the congregate shelters, many families are referred to welfare hotels where they typically are assigned their own room. These hotels often accept only short-term placements in order to avoid tenancy rights which allow families to stay for an indefinite period. Placement in these short-term hotels usually lasts from one night to 28 days after which the families must return to the EAU for another placement.

Welfare hotels provide a better environment for families with children in that they are given a private bedroom and may be allowed to stay for a longer term than in the congregate shelters. However, conditions are far from optimal in these hotels (Community Service Society of New York, 1984). Violence and criminal activities often make the hotels a dangerous place to live. Large families are often overcrowded in a single room without a refrigerator or cooking facilities. Furniture other than a bed is often lacking and the hotels are often in deteriorated condition.

Tier II transitional housing facilities. Congregate shelters and welfare hotels are often overcrowded and dangerous. Transitional housing facilities operated by nonprofit organizations appear to provide the best alternative for homeless families. In New York City transitional housing facilities are called Tier II shelters. Tier II shelters offer private family units and a relatively safe form of transitional housing. Many provide supportive services such as social work, counseling, job training and help locating housing. Lengths of stay in transitional housing can range from 4-6 months to as long as two years (Bassuk, 1990). There are relatively few such nonprofit shelters in the city. The shelter selected as the research setting for this study is a Tier II shelter.

Homelessness as a Trauma

Stress research has focused on people's reactions to trauma. Disasters such as floods, volcanoes, fire and war are examples of severe, catastrophic stressors that are outside the range of typical human experience. Losing one's home can be considered such a trauma. Exposure to traumatic events has been associated with a group of symptoms and reactions in people: post-traumatic stress disorder. Originally observed in veterans and war victims, the disorder has recently been acknowledged in children.

Post-traumatic stress disorder occurs following a catastrophic or extremely stressful event and includes persistent reexperiencing of the traumatic event and/or increased arousal (APA, 1987). Reexperiencing of the event may include recurrent recollections, repetitive play in young children involving traumatic themes, recurrent distressing dreams, avoidance of any reminders of the traumatic event including thoughts, feelings, activities and situations, loss of memory for parts of what happened, loss of interest in usual activities, loss of recently acquired developmental skills in young children, feelings of detachment from others, restricted range of affect and a sense of a foreshortened future.

Increased arousal is often exhibited through sleep disorders, angry outbursts, concentration difficulties, hypervigilance and/or an exaggerated startle response. Symptoms can occur immediately after the traumatic incident or begin six months or more afterwards.

In children, the most common symptoms of post-traumatic stress syndrome are sleep disorders, persistent thoughts of the event, fear that another similar event will occur, conduct problems, hyperalertness, avoidance of any reminder of the event, stress related physical symptoms and regression in young children to thumb-sucking, dependent behavior and enuresis (Frederick, 1985).

Homelessness and the Developmental Process

Erikson studied the importance of interactions with society and the environment in determining the way children and adults develop and experience themselves. He viewed human development as a series of life stages. A disruption at any of these stages is likely to have serious consequences. His theory seems particularly applicable to the study of mothers and children who have experienced homelessness. This section examines three of Erikson's life stages.

Erikson's (1963) fourth stage in the life cycle is "industry versus inferiority." He described the dominant virtue of this stage as "competence." He later went on to describe this period in the life cycle as follows: "Industriousness involves doing things beside and with others, a first sense of the division of labor. Competence, then, is the free exercise of dexterity and intelligence in the completion of serious tasks. It is the basis for cooperative participation in some segment of the culture" (1968, pp. 289-290).

Factors considered important in assessing this stage in children (Vaillant & Vaillant, 1981) are part-time jobs, household chores, participation in extracurricular activities, and school grades. In all societies children begin learning the tasks necessary for being adult members of society. In our society, this means being sent to school. If the child feels that he is learning these skills well, he or she will develop a sense of industry. However, if the child feels that he or she is not capable of performing these tasks and other children are, the child will develop a sense of inferiority.

The tasks of adolescence are different but equally important (Erikson, 1968). It is in this stage that adolescents begin to try to figure out who they are and what their role will be in society: identity versus role confusion. If he or she begins to be able to define their role and accompanying ideology, then he or she will develop an identity. If an adolescent is unable to resolve the identity crisis, he or she will develop a sense of role confusion. Adolescents may decide to identify with positive roles available within society such as various careers or more negative ones such as delinquency.

In adulthood a person is expected to become a productive, contributing member of society. When people feel they are successfully playing the role society expects from them, they will develop a sense of generativity. In contrast, if the person feels that he or she is not living up to society's expectations, they will develop a sense of stagnation.

HOMELESSNESS AND COPING SKILLS

Homelessness clearly places extraordinary demands on mothers and children. This section examines the various ways that individuals and families cope with these demands. Researchers have attempted to explain how people process catastrophic events. For example, Lindblad-Goldberg et al. (1988) found that a family's positive or negative perception of stressful events made a difference in their responses. Green, Wilson & Lindy (1985) proposed that several factors play a role in determining adaptation after stressful events. The first factor involves characteristics of the experience such as homelessness and would include variables such as change, loss and violence. The second factor involves how the person cognitively processes the event and whether they are able to assimilate the new information or whether they become overloaded and unable to process it. Green, Wilson and Lindy (1985) suggest that both individual characteristics such as age, sex and pre-existing stressors and the recovery environment which includes factors such as social supports affect how the individual processes the event. Finally, adaptation to the event occurs leading to either growth/coping or psychopathology/maladaptive response.

The Concept of Coping

Coping strategies allow people to avoid feelings of distress and maintain positive self-esteem (Menaghan, 1983). Lazarus and his colleagues (Lazarus, 1966; Lazarus & Folkman, 1984) have extensively researched and developed the concept of coping as a way of explaining stress reactions in individuals. They define coping as "constantly changing cognitive and behavioral efforts to manage specific external and/or internal demands that are appraised as taxing or exceeding the resources of the person" (Lazarus & Folkman, 1984, p. 141). According to these researchers coping has two major functions: to manage or alter the problem with the environment that causes distress (problem-focused coping), and to regulate the emotional response to distress (emotion-focused coping).

Central to this view of coping is the importance of perception or appraisal of a situation. Person-situation appraisals influence perception of events and coping strategies used. As people interact with the environment appraisals and coping strategies frequently shift and change.

In addition to cognitive appraisals and perceptions, many other factors have an impact on the coping experience. The ways people cope depend heavily on the resources available to them. Resources that have been found to enhance coping include health status, positive beliefs, problem solving skills, social skills, social support, and material resources (Lazarus & Folkman, 1984). Available resources are not always used due to personal constraints such as cultural or psychological values and beliefs and an unresponsive environment (Lazarus & Folkman, 1984).

Family Coping Strategies

The earliest researcher to generate a framework for examining the way families cope with a crisis was Hill (1949,1958). Hill developed a family crisis model called the ABCX model based on the three factors that interact when a family is faced with a stressful event and that determine whether the event will result in a family crisis. These factors are the stressor event (A), the family's crisis meeting resources (B) and the definition the family makes of the event (C) which interact to produce the family crisis (X).

More recent scholars of family stress and coping have found Hill's model somewhat limited as it focuses exclusively on pre-crisis variables that determine the family's ability to cope with a stressful event. McCubbin and Patterson (1983) elaborated on and adapted Hill's model to account for family adaptation to a stressful event over time and to focus on family resiliency and functional coping in the face of a crisis. In their adaptation, they attempt to integrate recent psychological (Lazarus, 1966; Mikhail, 1981) and physiological (Selye, 1974) research on people's reactions and adaptations to stress over time with Hill's sociological model. Post-crisis variables such as additional stressors and changes that occur after the event, psychological and social factors the family uses to cope and processes the family uses to achieve resolution have been added to the original model as they are thought to impact significantly on the family's ability to adapt and cope with a stressful event.

Figley (1983) attempted to identify functional and dysfunctional family coping patterns in response to stress . Families who cope in a functional manner can be differentiated from dysfunctional families by their ability to identify the stressor, to view the situation as a family problem rather than a problem of one or two members, adoption of a solution- oriented approach to difficulties rather than blaming others, showing tolerance for other family members, commitment and affection expressed among family members, open and clear communication among members, high family cohesion, role flexibility, appropriate utilization of resources inside and outside the family and lack of physical violence or substance abuse.

Children's Coping Strategies

One of the original and most comprehensive studies of coping strategies in children was undertaken by Murphy and others at the Menninger Foundation in Topeka, Kansas (Murphy, 1962; Murphy & Moriarty, 1976). They followed a group of children from the preschool years through adolescence, observing the children on a regular basis. They kept alert to naturally occurring stressful experiences in the children's lives and carefully noted and observed reactions to these events. Their study documented losses in the children's ordinary level of functioning, and observed their recovery to that level focusing on what coping strategies they used to maintain their equilibrium. Typical stresses faced by the children in the Topeka study included economic hardship, relocation, absence of mother, relatives' illness or stress, punishment, illnesses and others (Murphy, 1987).

Based on observations of many children, Murphy and her colleagues (Murphy & Moriarty, 1976) developed a profile of "good copers" who seemed to share a number of traits. These traits included "good feelings about themselves; good insights into interpersonal situations; realistic evaluations of the human and nonhuman environment; freewheeling attentiveness; flexibility with regards to means and ends; integration in their thinking, feeling, and acting; free translation of ideas into action; and marked intuition, originality and creativity (Murphy & Moriarty, 1976)." They also noted that "good copers" were able to "transform unpleasant reality through the medium of fantasy" and typically had parents who were models of resiliency themselves.

Murphy and Moriarity (1976) identified two types of coping techniques utilized by children. The first strategy consists of active problem solving and use of opportunities for an effective response to environmental demands, challenges, or obstacles. The second strategy consists of utilizing resources to keep from becoming too upset in response to these same demands.

Much of the recent research on factors that influence the way children cope with stress has come from researchers who were initially studying children considered at risk for emotional disorders. In their research they hoped to discover what factors placed children at risk and to identify the early signs of illness. In their work these researchers discovered a second group of children who did not succumb to mental illness despite conditions of adversity. The study of these resilient children has done much to illuminate the factors that seem to influence coping and adaptation to stress in children.

Children in several risk groups have been studied intensively including children of psychotic parents (Anthony, 1987; Garmezy, 1985); children in poverty (Werner & Smith, 1982; Werner, 1988; Felsman & Vaillant, 1988); children of divorce (Wallerstein & Kelly, 1980) as well as a sampling of the general population (Murphy & Moriarty, 1976). Several prospective longitudinal studies have followed and assessed children through adulthood and have begun to report adult outcome related to child competence. Researchers have begun to discover the coping strategies and other qualities these resilient children seem to share whether they are at risk because of environmental factors or due to a psychotic parent.

Many resilient children seem to learn to get what they need from other people if their parents are unavailable. Frequently they manage to form significant relationships with adults outside their family such as a teacher or clergy member who provide them with support and function as a role model (Werner, 1988; Garmezy, 1987). Family members such as grandparents and even the presence of a second parent when one parent is mentally ill can also function in these roles and can do much to ameliorate the impact of adversity (Werner, 1988; Fisher et al. 1987; Rutter, 1987; Anthony, 1974).

Another factor that seems to distinguish these resilient children from their more vulnerable peers is the ability to develop special interests or talents (Anthony, 1987; Bleuler, 1984; Werner, 1988). It does not seem to matter whether the child is exceptionally bright or gifted but that they use the ability or strengths they have to the utmost advantage. Several studies have noted that the more resilient children are more inner directed, autonomous and independent and not easily swayed by or influenced by the external environment (Space & Cromwell, 1978; Anthony, 1974; Werner, 1988).

The Role of Social Support in Mediating Stress

Social support has received much attention in the literature on stress. Such support has frequently been cited as a buffer against the detrimental effects of stress (Cobb, 1976; Unger & Powell, 1980). Belle (1982), in a study of low-income women, found that social support from family and friends related to child care assistance and emotional support was related to the women's emotional well being. However, social relationships also could bring with them additional stress and concerns such as when family or friends called upon the women for help with difficult problems such as alcoholism or abusive relationships.

Stack (1974) also found that social relationships for low-income women could be both positive and negative. In her study, she found women established support networks consisting of friends and relatives who helped each other with problems and crises. However, the women desperately needed to be part of the network for survival which led to some relationships which were forced and hostile as well as others that were positive and mutually beneficial.

III

Method

OVERVIEW

The purpose of this study was to explore and describe mothers' and school-age children's experience of and feelings about homelessness. The method was a qualitative, naturalistic inquiry. In-depth ethnographic interviews were conducted with six mothers and fourteen children.

In this chapter, the methods used to carry out the research are presented. Aspects of data collection are discussed, including preliminary research, selection of the research setting and research participants, the use of the in-depth interview, and the interview process. Analysis of the data is described, including procedures used to establish trustworthiness.

RATIONALE

The experiences and coping strategies of homeless mothers and children have been somewhat unexplored in the literature. Intensive study of selected examples has been demonstrated to be a particularly fruitful method for eliciting insights and generating hypotheses in areas where there has been little previous research to serve as a guide.

The orientation of qualitative research with its focus on people's meanings and understandings is congruent with the theoretical orientation of this study. The orientation, based primarily on the work of Lazarus (1966), has an underlying assumption that the stress of a given situation is subjective in nature and that the meanings or perceptions people hold will not only influence their experience but their coping behavior as well.

Similarly, the goal of qualitative methodology is to understand behavior from the subject's own frame of reference (Bogdan & Bicklen, 1984). Qualitative methodology seeks to understand the way participants have organized their world including their thoughts about what is happening, their experiences, and their basic perceptions (Patton, 1980). With the qualitative techniques of small sample size and in-depth interviewing, a rich, full description of the perceptions and coping strategies of mothers and children who have experienced homelessness was obtained.

PROCEDURE

Selection of Research Setting

The shelter in which the study was conducted is a Tier II facility located in a low income neighborhood in New York City. It is operated by a nonprofit organization and houses eighty families in three semi-detached buildings. One building is reserved for battered women and their children with a maximum length of stay of ninety days. Such families were not included in the present study. In the other two buildings, the shelter accepts homeless families with children without regard for the circumstances that led up to their homelessness. Families are accepted as residents depending on the availability of space. The average length of stay in this facility is eight or nine months.

This shelter is similar to other Tier II facilities. The shelter provides private apartments with kitchen facilities and offers many support services. Each family in the shelter is assigned a social worker who helps them to locate permanent housing and to cope with other difficulties. Families also have the option to participate in many support and educational groups run by the shelter. The shelter offers a job training program and a GED preparation course and provides recreational services such as a day camp for children during the summer months.

The shelter selected as the setting for this study is one of several operated by nonprofit organizations in New York City. Directors of several such shelters were contacted. Some shelters were inappropriate because they only served mothers with preschool children and did not have the targeted population of school age children. Other shelter directors were uninterested in participating and were unwilling to discuss the project. The director of the selected shelter requested a brief description of the proposed study and agreed to participate after receiving it. She designated her assistant as the primary contact person for the research project.

Research Participants

The research participants in this study were six homeless Black or Hispanic families who resided temporarily in the selected Tier II facility. The participants met the following criteria for selection:

1. Families were female-headed households.
2. Families received public assistance.
3. Families had at least one child between the ages of 5 and 13.
4. Families had lived in the current shelter for at least 3 months
5. Family members spoke English

Participants included families who were in the shelter for at least three months and were limited to English-speaking, Black or Hispanic female headed families receiving public assistance with at least one child in the 5-13 year old age range. This is an important group to select for research as single, minority mothers with minor children comprise the largest group of homeless families (Citizen's Committee for Children of New York, 1988). Since the researcher is monolingual the families included in the study were limited to those who spoke English.

For the purposes of this study, families are defined as a family configuration headed by a single woman and including her dependent children who currently live with her. Homeless families are considered to be families who lack a permanent place of residence but currently reside in a short term temporary shelter.

The technique of purposive sampling was used in this study to obtain participants (Bogden & Bicklen, 1982; Lincoln & Guba, 1985). This type of sampling allows the researcher to select participants purposively to reflect the goals of the research project. Purposive sampling also increases the chances that a full range of views will be exposed and that multiple realities will be discovered (Guba & Lincoln, 1981).

TABLE I
Participating Families

NAME	AGE	CHILDREN	AGES	TIME IN SYSTEM
Michelle Michaels	34	Jennifer John Robert Julissa Ricky	13 11 9 7 4	8 months
Maria Perez	30	Annie Elizabeth Michael	11 10 4	3 years
Linda Garcia	33	Jimmy Erica	11 3	11 months
Evelyn Smith	35	Dana Cindy	12 6	16 months
Isabel Gonzalez	40	Jose Christina	13 11	15 months
Sylvia Jones	24	Alison Diana Jason Lisa	8 6 5 3	4 1/2 months

The research sample was kept small to provide the richest, fullest description of the experience of these mothers and children. Sampling toward redundancy (Guba & Lincoln, 1981) is a concept frequently used in determining sample size in qualitative research. The basic premise is that sampling should continue until new interviews provide little new or additional information. In this dissertation this concept was necessarily applied in a limited manner. Some flexibility in sample size was expected. It was anticipated that the number of families selected would range from four to eight, depending on the number of children in each family and the redundancy of the interviews. Six families were eventually selected.

Participants were recruited through the distribution of a flier describing the project. Families were offered twenty-five dollars for participation to increase motivation to participate. The decision to pay families a small fee for participation was made after consultation with the director and assistant director at the shelter who felt that a monetary incentive would increase the mother's willingness to participate. They were asked to complete and return an information form to the front desk at the shelter if interested in participation.

Sixteen families volunteered to participate in the study, and all were contacted. In some cases the families were screened out because the mother did not speak English or because they were not female-headed households. Other families were eliminated because they did not have children in the targeted age range. Since more families were interested in participating than needed for the study an attempt was made to achieve diversity by selecting three Hispanic and three Black families. In addition, although it was not possible to obtain equal numbers of boys and girls an, attempt was made to come as close as possible with the available pool of families. Families not selected were notified after the final group was selected.

For the families selected to participate, parents and children were informed about the purpose of the study and the need for at least two audiotaped interviews. They were assured of the anonymity and confidentiality of their interviews and told that the tapes would be erased after they were transcribed. Written permission was sought from the mothers for their own and their children's participation before proceeding with the interviews. Parents and children were told that they could have access to written or oral feedback on the results of this research. They were also told that they withdraw from the study at any time, without repercussions.

Data Collection

The data collected were verbatim transcripts of audiotaped ethnographic interviews. Another important source of data was the researcher's field notes.

The ethnographic interview. A major tool of qualitative methodology is the in-depth or ethnographic interview. The ethnographic interview has long been used by social scientists such as anthropologists and sociologists and has more recently become popular with psychologists and educators (Spradley, 1979). The name ethnographic interview reveals its origins in ethnography, anthropology and the study of culture.

According to Ely (1984) the goal of the ethnographic interviewer is "to understand and describe the meanings people hold. In striving to come closer to understanding people's meanings, the ethnographic interviewer learns from people as informants and seeks to discover the information they use to organize their behavior"(p. 4). This type of interview promotes "guided conversation" by encouraging the interviewees to speak freely about their perceptions and thoughts as they relate to the research topic (Agar, 1980; Lofland & Lofland, 1984). The purpose of this study was to describe and understand the way homeless mothers and children make sense of their environment and how their thoughts and perceptions affect their coping behaviors. The ethnographic interview was an effective means to achieve this purpose.

Following guidelines set forth by ethnographic interviewers (Spradley, 1979; Whyte, 1984; Guba & Lincoln, 1981), participants were encouraged to describe their experience in their way. Beginning questions were designed with the research focus on perceptions and coping in mind (see Appendix A for a list of guiding questions). As the interviews progressed, the interviewer tried to phrase additional questions in a flexible manner to best understand the participant's experience. The interview differs from more structured interviews in it's flexibility, and "is designed to provide the informant with the freedom to introduce material that were not anticipated by the interviewer" (Whyte, 1984, p. 97).

Several techniques have been described by researchers familiar with in-depth interviewing as ways of helping participants express themselves during interviews. These techniques were applied in a flexible manner during the interviews conducted for this study. Spradley (1979) suggests that children as young as first grade may make good informants and participants in ethnographic interviews. Initially, it is important to develop rapport with the subject (Whyte, 1984). Unless the interviewee feels comfortable they are unlikely to reveal their thoughts and feelings freely. It is important for the interviewer not to criticize or pass judgment on the subject's opinions or thoughts (Guba & Lincoln, 1981). Therefore, the first questions focused on "breaking the ice" with the participants and concentrated on current activities and interests that were thought to be somewhat easy to discuss. The topic of homelessness was introduced later.

Both the phrasing and sequencing of questions have been found to influence the interview process. Spradley (1979) suggests three types of questions for the ethnographic interview: descriptive, structural and contrast. All three types of questions were integrated into the interviews with the mothers and children. His recommendation to begin with descriptive questions that, as the name implies, encourage respondents to provide broad descriptions was followed. In certain cases with the children, his suggestion of asking respondents to draw a picture or map of the place they are describing was followed which greatly facilitated information provided. Following this suggestion, an example of a possible descriptive question posed to the children was, "Draw a picture of where you lived before and tell me about what it was like."

According to Lincoln and Guba (1981), the sequencing of questions in an interview also can significantly affect the subject's response. They suggest two types of sequencing described as the funnel and inverted funnel. The funnel sequence involves starting with more open-ended questions and gradually moving toward more specific ones. It is advantageous because it gives the subject an opportunity to warm up and relax in the presence of the interviewer. However, not all subjects are comfortable beginning with an open-ended general question, particularly when they are not fully committed to the interview process, are shy or feel they do not understand exactly what is required (Guba and Lincoln, 1981). In such cases Guba and Lincoln recommend use of the inverted funnel sequence of questions in which the interviewer begins with specific questions and moves to more general open- ended ones toward the end of the interview when the subject feels more comfortable and confident. The funnel and inverted funnel sequence of questions were applied during this study on a case by case basis depending on how the participants responded to the interview.

Whyte (1984) also has several suggestions for successful interviewing. He recommends probes posed by the interviewer after the interviewee's response and suggests that these will increase elaboration and exploration of topics. His first suggestion involves probing the last statement made by a subject by asking a question or posing a comment directly related to it or commenting on it. His second suggestion involves asking more about topics brought up earlier in the interview either directly preceding the last idea mentioned or even going further back to a topic that wasn't fully explored earlier in the interview. Lastly he recommends introducing a new topic that hasn't been explored yet. All Whyte's (1984) techniques were used during the interviews in this study.

Interview setting. Interviews took place at times and locations chosen as convenient by the participants. All participants chose to have the interviews take place in their apartments. They were told that the setting for the interview should be sufficiently quiet so that the interview could proceed without interruption and so that a tape-recorder could be used to record the session. Most families were able to provide a quiet space either in the kitchen or a bedroom. In some cases it was necessary to use a somewhat quiet corner of the living room when there was no other available space. An attempt was made to conduct the interviews in a somewhat private place so that the participants would feel free to discuss their thoughts and feelings in confidence without the presence of others.

Interview schedule. Interviews with participants usually took place in two sessions lasting approximately forty-five minutes to one hour. Some interviews with the children were shorter. Most participants were interviewed at least twice. In a few cases children refused a second interview and the first was used. The second interview took place several days or weeks after the first. After the first interview the interviewer listened to the tape several times before returning for a second interview to determine areas that need further clarification and questioning.

Preliminary field trial. Preliminary interviews were conducted with a mother and child in one family group that helped with refinement of initial interview questions and technique. But, since the interviews were rich and the mother had four children within the age range for the study it was decided to consider the family as the first participants.

Field notes. The researcher kept detailed field notes that were written soon after each interview was completed. The notes contained impressions and reflections on the interview, participant and the setting as recommended by Bogdan and Bicklen (1982). These notes were used to supplement and clarify the interview material.

Data Analysis

The goal of the qualitative data analysis was to identify major patterns and themes that emerged from interviews with the research participants. Regularities and patterns in the data were developed into a category system that served to organize the findings (Bogdan & Bicklen, 1982). The purpose of this category system was to integrate the data and to increase understanding of the participants' experience (Ely, 1984). To avoid losing much of the richness, meaning and detail that characterizes qualitative research methodology, no preexisting category system was imposed on the data (Ely, 1984; Whyte, 1984).

The goal of categorizing the data into themes was to arrive at a coding system that was exhaustive and used all the transcribed material (Weiss, 1968). New categories were developed until all data deemed relevant were accounted for satisfactorily. Bogdan and Bicklin (1982) provide some guidelines and suggestions for developing coding categories that include: descriptions of the setting/context, definitions of the situation, perspectives or shared understandings, understandings of people and things in the environment, process or changes over time, regularly occurring activities or behavior, strategies people use to accomplish things and relationships or social networks. These categories were used as a starting point for developing coding categories that fit the data collected in this study (See Appendix B for the list of coding categories).

After the interviews were transcribed, data were analyzed according to methods described and elaborated by Ely (1984) and Ely, Anzul, Friedman, Garner and Steinmetz (1991). After repeatedly listening to the tapes and reading the transcripts, preliminary impressions and patterns in the data were noted. The researcher then began to formulate tentative themes or categories that emerged from the data. Themes were selected either based on meaningful statements that were repeated in many interviews or powerful factual or emotional statements that occurred less frequently but had high impact (Ely, 1984). Themes were formulated from the actual content of the interview as well as based on the theoretical orientation of the study (Bussis, Chittenden & Amarel, 1976). After this, categories were refined and clarified by reviewing the data and the relationship between impressions and tentative categories. Interview data was coded into categories after categories were assigned numbers and subcategories assigned a letter suffix. Transcripts were marked with the codes as appropriate. During this phase new impressions were noted and coding categories further refined. Coded data from the transcripts were sorted into similar categories and listed together. A microcomputer and word processing program were used to simplify this task.

Results of coding were studied and new impressions and categories noted. Statements in similar categories were organized into themes. Data on each participant were integrated in order to clarify the full range of information available. Profiles of each participant were developed. Finally, comparisons were made between individual participants and family groups (See Appendix B for a list of the categories and themes developed for this study).

The goal of categorizing the data into themes is to arrive at a coding system that is exhaustive and uses all the transcribed material (Weiss, 1968). New categories were developed until all data was accounted for in a satisfactory manner. Bogdan and Bicklen (1982) provide guidelines and suggestions for developing coding categories. An adaptation of Bogdan and Bicklen's (1982) categories that seemed particularly relevant to this study will be described below and were used as a starting point for developing coding categories that fit the data collected in this study.

Strategy codes refer to the tactics, methods, ways, techniques, maneuvers, ploys, and other conscious ways people accomplish various things. Strategy codes were particularly important in this study as coping strategies fit under this category. In fact, this description of strategy codes provides a good working definition of coping strategies that was used throughout data collection and analysis.

Setting/context codes include general statements people make describing the subject, the setting and how the setting fits in the community.

Definition of the situation codes refers to how the participants define the setting or particular topic. Of particular interest was their view of the world and how they see themselves in relation to the setting and their situation.

Subject's ways of thinking about people and objects include codes that capture their understanding of each other, of outsiders, and of the objects that make up their world.

Process codes refer to words or phrases that categorize sequences of events, changes over time and passages from one type of status to another.

Establishing Trustworthiness

Researcher bias, premature interpretation of data without sufficient evidence, and over reliance on data from some informants while ignoring data from other participants can all jeopardize the trustworthiness of the results of qualitative research (Bogdan and Bicklen, 1982; Lincoln and Guba, 1985; Miles & Huberman, 1984).

Several techniques were used to increase the trustworthiness of this study.

Prolonged engagement. An attempt was made to increase credibility by spending enough time with participants to build trust and to gain an understanding of the context in which the interviews took place. This technique was used to minimize distortions and misunderstandings.

Interview technique. Since the ethnographic interview was the primary research instrument in this study, credibility depends heavily on the interviewer following guidelines for such interviews. To improve interview technique a research colleague trained and experienced in in-depth interviewing technique listened to and critiqued three ten-minute segments of the preliminary field interviews.

Triangulation. Credibility can be increased through crossvalidation of information from different sources or through different methods (Miles & Huberman, 1984; Guba & Lincoln, 1981). In this study triangulation occurred through comparison of informal observation of family behavior and ensuing notes with information obtained through the interviews. In addition, family members were asked to provide information about other members that was compared to data provided by individual members on their experience.

Negative cases. Credibility can be increased if the researcher is careful to search through the data for negative cases that do not easily fit into the established themes or categories (Lincoln & Guba, 1985). Negative cases force the researcher to refine and reorganize categories and themes until the negative cases can be explained or accounted for (Guba & Lincoln, 1981; Miles & Huberman, 1984). Through examination and analysis of negative cases the researcher was able to revise themes to account for all important findings.

Research group. The researcher was part of a group of other doctoral students using qualitative methodology in their dissertation work. Meetings with fellow qualitative researchers were an important part of data analysis and provided an opportunity to test working hypotheses in addition to helping the researcher question biases, explore meanings and clarify interpretations on an ongoing basis (Guba & Lincoln, 1981). Although many group members changed over the course of the study, the researcher met on a regular basis with one other doctoral student throughout the project. This colleague was given several interviews to code both during the development of the categories and after they were more established. In both cases we worked together until the level of agreement was high.

Feedback from participants. Obtaining feedback from the research participants is important for enhancing credibility of qualitative studies (Lincoln & Guba, 1985). In this study, checking back with the respondents was ongoing. Follow-up interviews served this purpose and were used for clarification and elaboration of information obtained during the first interview as well as to obtain additional information. The second interviews also gave the researcher an opportunity to correct interpretations and to check her understanding of the participants point of view (Lincoln & Guba, 1985).

The researcher shared some results of the data analysis with two of the original participants. She read the list of group theme headings to them and asked if the statements made sense. The participants agreed that the themes credibly described either their views of those of others they knew while at the shelter.

IV

Results: Family Profiles

This chapter presents the results of the first level of analysis through descriptive profiles of families who participated in the study. Using a combination of narrative and direct quotations, each profile begins with an introduction to the mother and her children. It continues with a description of their experience of homelessness. Profiles include each individual's response to being in the study, family history, and a description of how the family became homeless. To ensure confidentiality, all names and other identifying information have been changed.

INTRODUCTION TO THE MICHAELS FAMILY

The Michaels family consists of Michelle and her five children, Jennifer, age 12, John, age 11, Robert, age 9, Julissa, age 6, and Ricky, age 4. They are a Black family who have been in the shelter system for eight months. They spent one week in a barracks shelter, four months in a hotel, and have been in the current shelter for four months. Michelle is currently involved with a man who is not the father of any of her children. He was often there during my visits and appeared to be staying with the family.

The Michaels family lives in a two bedroom apartment. The children sleep in the bedrooms while Michelle sleeps in the living room on a sofabed. Although she had closed her bed and straightened up the living room on my first visit, on subsequent visits the living room was crowded with the bed open. There was a television which was almost always on. The children had bicycles, but few other toys.

Michelle and her four oldest children were interviewed for the study. Interviews took place in the kitchen of their apartment where it was possible to obtain some privacy and quiet. All family members were interviewed at least twice and several visits were necessary to complete all the interviews. Interviews were scheduled over a period of two months. The Michaels family was the first to be interviewed and was originally considered the pilot for the study. However, the interviews went well and yielded so much information that it was decided to include them in the study.

Profile of Michelle Michaels

Michelle as a participant in the study. Michelle is a 34 year old woman who grew up in New York City with her maternal grandmother. Her mother, an alcoholic who physically abused Michelle, died when Michelle was 12 years old. Michelle has no siblings. She said she dropped out of high school against her grandmothers wishes because she wanted to work. She married her first husband soon after and had her first two children, Jennifer and John. Her husband also physically abused her, and he eventually left her. She said that he is currently in jail. Soon after she became involved with the father of her last three children. However, he is married to another woman who also has three children with him. Michelle continues to see him but claims that she ended the relationship last week. She felt he was too demanding and also fought with and hit her. He has a job and gives her money for the children on an irregular basis. He also visits the children fairly regularly. Currently Michelle is involved with another man who she has known for a few years. He has been staying with her for the past few weeks and helps watch the children. He is not employed.

When I arrived for the first visit Michelle was dressed nicely and had taken special care with her appearance since she was being interviewed. She had cleaned the apartment and rearranged the living room into a sitting area. However, on subsequent visits her appearance was less polished. Michelle was interviewed three times. While her first interview took place in the living room the second and third took place in the kitchen.

Michelle seemed very anxious during the first interview and spoke almost nonstop for an hour. She smoked throughout the interviews. She readily shared information about her situation, her family, and life in general. She spoke openly about all areas but switched quickly from topic to topic. Michelle initially believed I was a psychiatrist and seemed to want to discuss all her difficulties. After I reassured her that I was not a psychiatrist and clarified the purpose of the research, she seemed to approach the second interview more calmly. I also learned from the first interview that it was important to structure her somewhat so that I would get information on the research topic.

At the time of the last interview the Michaels family had just received word that they would be moving to an apartment in a public housing project in the city. They were all very excited about moving.

Michelle's experience. Michelle and her children lived in an apartment in the Bronx for many years. She said she was using crack and had bought it on credit from drug dealers. She was unable to repay her debt and was harassed and threatened by them. She said she decided to leave the apartment before she or her children were hurt. Michelle stayed with friends and relatives before entering the shelter system. She said:

> When I gave up my apartment, me and the children went and stayed with my boyfriend's mother. It started out okay but it ended up like a terror. I don't know. It couldn't work. Me and her just couldn't get along. We argued and stuff I never really cursed out no old person unless they did it to me and I tried to avoid it unless they had pushed me and that's how she was. And then when things didn't go her way, she told us to get out. So I just left. And I'm glad she did put me out cause if she hadn't I'd probably still be there going through hell with her.

Next, she found a place for her family in a friend's building in Brooklyn. She described that place:

> We had moved back to Brooklyn with this lady I knew, this building I used to live in, a house. She gave us two rooms down in her basement. That was horrible. Because we had to move our bowels, pee in a bucket. We had no running water, no cooking facilities. I had to pay somebody to go in their apartment to use the bathroom, to empty the bucket and sometimes they didn't want you to, so this was backing up. We had rats. Everything. This was a basement.

After leaving that basement, Michelle went to stay with her grandmother. She explained why this was also problematic:

> We went and stayed with my grandmother for a
> couple of days. She only had three rooms and I
> don't know. She claimed the kids was always
> getting on her nerves. I couldn't go no where. You
> know the kids could be sleep and I wanted to go to
> the store, I and went to a shelter.

Michelle and her children were initially sent to a large barracks
shelter where they stayed for seven days. She described what it was
like at the shelter:

> It wasn't even a room. Just a big community room
> with everybody. You got families here, a man and
> wife here, me and my kids was in the middle of
> the floor, six beds. We had one locker. You had
> to watch your stuff because they would go in your
> locker and take your stuff. They didn't care even if
> you had a lock on it. I was supposed to stay there
> 21 days. I was lucky. I got out there in 7 days.

Michelle asked to leave the barracks shelter after witnessing a
fight among residents. She said:

> But what happened was they had a fight there one
> night on my floor and I didn't like it so I asked the
> man. I was trying to get a Tier II like this at first
> but he said he didn't have none. I had just missed
> one but he had a hotel that I could go to.

Michelle liked the hotel much better. She said,

> It was okay. It was nice because I got along with
> the managers. Like if you wanted to go out the
> managers would watch the children, they would
> make sure nothing would go wrong. That's the type
> of people they were. They didn't have to be like
> that. It was nice I liked it. If we had to stay there
> I would have stayed because it didn't cause no
> problems. I didn't have any. If you didn't want to
> be bothered with nobody you just stayed in your
> room and nobody be messing with you. It was like
> a big private house. It wasn't like those big hotels
> in the middle of the city. I'm glad they didn't send

> me no place like that. It was nice. When we first
> got there it was like heaven to be able to sleep on
> a comfortable bed and have privacy.

Michelle said her children seemed to like the hotel:

> They liked it. My oldest daughter she found her
> another boyfriend there. Every where she goes she
> find her a boyfriend. They liked it. My sons they
> had little friends around there. They liked the
> schools they were going to.

Michelle spoke favorably about the current shelter:

> I mean I respect myself more. I feel much better
> about myself. At one time I wanted to put the kids
> away and go lock myself in a hospital some place
> because I felt I couldn't take it no more. Since I
> been here it hasn't bothered me. It's like I'm more
> prepared to deal with them now and life too. I'm
> more content and ready.

She reported that the staff at the shelter have helped her to change:

> Until they put me someplace permanent I have my
> own apartment again. That's a big difference
> because we was like in two little rooms in the
> hotel and I mean they were small too. . . I'm just
> more content here. And like I said here I've been
> getting involved in a lot of things, like the school,
> working when I first came. I used to be lazy in the
> hotel. Since I been here, my social worker can tell
> you, she said I make her job easy for her. Cause I
> just go out and do things and then come back and
> tell her. She's like I was just going to suggest that
> but I already go and do it. I make sure they go to
> school and I jump right up and do whatever I have
> to do and come back. Like I'm bored now because
> I don't have anything to do. Before it didn't bother
> me at all. I just lay right down all day and watch
> the stories on television and I didn't care.

Michelle found a job at the shelter soon after she arrived. She worked providing child care for parents who were attending meetings. However, at the time of the second interview she decided to return to school to earn her high school equivalency and to obtain training for a job in medical assistance. Michelle was very positive about starting school and attended regularly for two months. However, at the time of the third interview she decided to take a leave of absence because she needed to supervise her children who were home from school for the summer.

Although Michelle said that she has stopped using drugs, she said that she does drink on a regular basis. She said, "sometimes I need a drink. The pressure gets to me. I don't want to go crazy. Not until I raise them up anyway. And lots of times I feel like that's what's gonna happen to me."

Michelle reported that her family has not been very supportive since she became homeless. Her grandmother and cousins are reluctant to help her financially, and she feels they think she should be able to survive on the money she receives from welfare. Her grandmother did not want her to stay with her when she had no place to go, but does give her some money once in a while. She does not understand her grandmother's reluctance to help since her great grandchildren are involved. Michelle helps her grandmother with her shopping and other errands on a regular basis.

Profile of Jennifer Michaels

Jennifer as a participant in the study. Jennifer is a pretty thirteen year old Black girl who looks older than her stated age. She was in her bedroom with her boyfriend watching television during my visits with the family. On the first visit she left her boyfriend somewhat reluctantly so that she could be interviewed. However, she agreed to participate and signed the consent form.

Jennifer was interviewed twice. She was somewhat guarded about discussing her experience but was able to express her opinions in a forthright manner particularly as she grew more comfortable during the first interview. While Jennifer's mood was upbeat during the first interview she seemed unhappy and depressed during the second. She did not want to discuss her feelings and said she was too tired to talk so the interview was short. However, her mother later told me that her boyfriend had been in a fight with another boy who lived in the shelter and had been cut with a knife. He received stitches and was recovering but was no longer allowed to visit Jennifer at the shelter.

Jennifer's experience. Jennifer described a strong emotional response to leaving their old apartment. She said:

> I felt nauseous. It was bad. I didn't want to move.
> Then we had to stay in other peoples houses. And
> we couldn't do what we want to do like we used to
> do in our apartment.

She said she does not remember leaving because, "It's too much." She added the hardest thing for her was "the moving every time, 24 hours, 7 days a week." Jennifer remembered feeling "mad" when her mother told her they were moving.

Jennifer said that she thought the shelter was "alright" and wanted to stay because she had a boyfriend there. She also said she liked to watch the large color television in the lounge. However, she was adamant in her dislike for the food. She said, "It was nasty. I never used to eat shelter food. I didn't like the way it looked. I didn't like the way people was talking about it. Babies got sick from the milk." Instead, she said that she would wait for her mother to buy food at the supermarket. Jennifer also complained that the shelter was dirty and there were "rats running around everybody's beds."

Jennifer's memories of the hotel are not very positive. She recalled getting into a fight with a sixteen year old who was "starting trouble" with her. She said, "once I knew she wanted to fight me so I fought her. I beat her upstairs and downstairs." She said she also felt good about leaving the hotel because, "There was a lot of boys who wanted to go with me. Just because I didn't want to go with them they used to talk about me." She said she had a boyfriend and "All of the boys wanted my boyfriend to fight them. So I just wasn't around too much."

Jennifer reported that she felt more positive about the current shelter because she likes the neighborhood and her school. She also has a boyfriend whom she likes very much and spends most of her time with after school and on weekends. She said that things are going better for her than in the past because she stays in the apartment and does not go outside often. She worried that her behavior might cause the shelter to evict her family and does not want to leave. She said:

> I don't go outside because there's trouble. Girls
> start with you. You get in the wrong crowd. So I

don't go outside. I see they start with other kids
then I figure they'll start with me. Then I might
have to fight and get my mother put out so I just
stay upstairs. Cause I'm tough. If someone messes
with my brothers or says something about my
mother I'll fight them. So that's why I stay upstairs
out of trouble. I only go to school and when I go to
school at lunch time that's the only time I go
outside. Or I go to the store for my mother.

Jennifer is currently in sixth grade but should be in eighth grade.
She blamed her failure to be promoted on the family's frequent
moves and her tardiness. Jennifer also felt that her behavior was a
factor in her not being promoted. She said she was fidgety and
talked back to teachers. She said for example,

If a teacher talked back to me. I talk back to her.
And if she say something smart, I say something
smart. And if one kid bothers me in my class and I
tell him to leave me alone once and they bother
me twice, then I get out of hand.

Jennifer feels more positively about her current school than she
had about other schools she attended in the past. She said, "I like
the school. I like the teacher." She said that she is trying to do
well in school and would like to catch up so that she would be in
the correct grade. Her boyfriend helps her with her school work. She
asks her teacher to give her extra work to do on the weekends.

Jennifer reported that her boyfriend is very supportive and he
seemed to be her only friend. She said:

After school and on the weekends I just stay in the
house and play cards with my friend. We have
money and we bring in stuff to eat. We look at
TV. We write stuff on paper. We do math. We do
spelling.

She added that everyone in her family likes him and he helps all of
them:

He play with us. He bring games over for us to
play. He nice. He help my brothers with their
homework. He help all of us. He help my mother.

My mother ask him to clean the house and he do
it. He do a lot of things for us.

Jennifer said that the most important people to her are her
mother and sister and brothers, "cause I love them." Since she is
the oldest, Jennifer watches her siblings when her mother is out.
She also helps her mother in other ways, "I clean for her, cook for
her. I do a lot of things. I give her money."

Jennifer travels by herself to visit friends and relatives. She
visits her godfather, uncle, father, stepmother, godmother and
grandmother. However, she has managed to keep her situation
secret from many of her old friends and said, "Nobody knows I'm out
here at the shelter except for my godfather, my grandmother, my
uncles. My friends don't."

Profile of Julissa Michaels

Julissa as a participant in the study. Julissa is a pretty seven year
old girl who is thin and tall for her age. She eagerly agreed to be
interviewed and seemed very excited. She was interested in the
tape recorder and wanted to hear her voice played back on the tape.
She spoke freely and seemed to enjoy talking with the interviewer.
However, she sometimes had difficulty explaining her experience
and the use of crayons and paper helped her to recall and to
describe her experience. Julissa was interviewed twice with the
second interview used to obtain additional information and provide
clarification regarding information provided in the first interview.

Julissa's experience. Julissa recalled when her mother told her
they were leaving their old apartment. She said, "I told all my
friends bye. I felt a little bit sad." She remembered her cats and
dogs, her cousin who went to school with her and her uncles' store
that was a few blocks from where they lived. She says that she
goes back to see her friends with her sister.

Julissa said that she liked the shelter her family stayed in. She
said,

> We could run around. It was a nice place. Cause
> you could make you a lot of friends there because
> they got too much people. I didn't want to leave
> cause that was a nice place.

She also said she liked the hotel and did not want to leave there
either. She said,

> That was kind of nice too. It had fire escapes.
> And they had some parties. It was a nice house.
> And me and my sister had us some boyfriends. . .
> We used to go outside, go to the parks. Play
> nicely. We played basketball and we found some
> toys.

However, Julissa's favorite place to stay is her father's house.
She said, "I want to go to his house everyday cause he buy us stuff
and he take care of us. Like my mommy do."

Julissa seemed happy in the current shelter. She said that she
has many friends in school and the shelter with whom she plays
with afterschool and on weekends. She said,

> I like to play school with them. Play nicely with
> them. I draw with them. I color with them. I see
> some of them outside. When I come home from
> school I ask my mother could I go outside. Could I
> take out my bike? She says, "yeah" and I ride
> some of my friends on it.

However, Julissa does not like the rats she says she has seen in
their shelter apartment.

Julissa is in first grade and according to her mother is doing
well in school. At the time of my last interview with the family,
she had been promoted to second grade. She has a positive attitude
towards school. She said,

> I like to learn, math, math books, reading, working
> in a workbook. Going to school every day. . . I
> listen to my teacher so I could learn work.

Profile of John Michaels

John as a participant in the study. John is a friendly, good
looking eleven year old boy. He was interviewed after his seven
year old sister at the kitchen table in his family's apartment at the
shelter. Although John willingly agreed to participate he seemed to
be in a rush to meet his friends outside to play ball. He called to
them several times out of the window.

John was sincere and spoke frankly about his experience. However, he spoke slowly and used few words. He drew pictures with crayons while being interviewed. John was interviewed twice with the second interview primarily for clarification of topics covered in the first interview.

John's experience. John clearly described his family's reasons for leaving their old apartment. He said:

> They used to sell drugs over there. And we had a
> fight, my mother and my family had this fight with
> another family and my mother got tired of it. Then
> she left.

He said he felt sad when he left "because I had cousins that live on the second floor from me and my friends in my class and stuff." When his mother told him they were moving he added, "I got mad. I just went out of the house and think. Then we left." He said that he occasionally returns to his old neighborhood with his sister to visit his cousins.

John recalled leaving their apartment and staying with his Aunt Sue. He explained that she's not really his aunt but they call her that "because she's nice to us." He said there were some problems because, "my mother and her, they argue sometimes." After leaving Aunt Sue's he recalled moving to the barracks shelter. He said, "It was a little bit nice. We made a lot of friends there." However, he wanted to leave, "because you can't have your own privacy and everybody got to share the bathroom. I didn't like it." John preferred the hotel his family was sent to after the shelter. He said, "It was alright. We could go to the beach and the sand. We could catch fish in there." When asked how he felt when he left the hotel he said, "I still left sad because it was like a home." John also likes the current shelter and said, "It's nice too." He said that he has many friends who live in the shelter or surrounding area, " all these buildings right here I got friends and in the projects too."

John is an avid baseball and basketball player. He said, "I play baseball for three hours and I play basketball for three hours cause I want to practice. I want to be on the baseball team." John said that a coach comes to the park where he plays to ask if anyone wants to be on a team, and he practices every day in the hopes that he will be chosen. Right now he said he just plays with his friends in the park near the shelter. He usually plays outside until it gets dark.

After school, John works in the supermarket. He said that he usually earns around six dollars. He described what he does, "I pack people's bags up and if there's a lot of bags I put it in their shopping cart and help them to their house. And they give me money for doing it." When John earns money he said, "I give some to my mother. Like if I have ten dollars I give her most of it to buy food and stuff."

According to his mother, John is in a class for learning disabled children in school. She said that he was born prematurely and always seemed to learn more slowly than her other children. However, he is doing well in his class and may be mainstreamed in the future. Like his siblings, John has been in three different schools since his family became homeless. However, John seems to have a fairly positive attitude towards school. He said that he thinks his teacher is nice and explained "we go on trips then we write about it then we draw about it. Then we make stuff. Today we had to make flowers. Then we play games and go to lunch." He said that he preferred some of the other schools he went to because he was given more play time.

Profile of Robert Michaels

Robert as a participant in the study. Robert is a handsome nine year old boy who is more reserved than his siblings. He was interviewed in the kitchen after his older brother, John. He frequently answered questions with yes or no and often said that he did not know. It was usually necessary to rephrase questions several times in order to obtain a response. He was interviewed twice with most information obtained during the first interview. The second served mainly for clarification.

Robert's experience. Robert said that he was glad to leave their old apartment:

> It be fights around there, and it's nasty around there
> and people start too much trouble around there.
> And my mother moved out.

When asked how he felt when his mother told him they were moving he said, "I said nothing. I was happy. Because I been wanting to move out of there." He recalled one fight in particular:

> My mother was fighting with this lady. She lived
> in the same building. First my big sister had a
> fight with her big daughter. And then my sister's
> other friend went and told my mother and her
> mother thought my mother was gonna hit on her
> daughter. And then they start fighting and then my
> uncle came and broke it up. . . People was calling
> the cops. They asked my mom to come to the
> precinct and she said no and she just went in the
> house. All of us went in the house.

After leaving their apartment, Robert said they went to his
stepmother's house (the mother of the man with whom his mother is
involved). He said, "It was fun. We played." When asked why
they left there he said,

> Cause one day when we was asleep, her and my
> mother had an argument. And then she waked us
> up and tell us to come on. And she called my
> father and tell him to come pick us up. He took us
> home with him and we stayed there until tomorrow.

Robert felt "bad" when they left "cause they were arguing and we
was sleeping."

Robert recalled leaving his father's home and moving in with
his grandmother. He said it was "okay" there because "my mother
never got into no arguments." While there he said he went to the
park and played with his brothers and sisters. He said they left their
grandmother's house "Cause we had to go to the shelter. Cause my
mother and father went looking for one."

Robert clearly disliked the barracks shelter where his family
was first sent. He said he did not like, "the rats going in people's
food and sneaking in people's stuff when they be sleep." He said
there was nothing he liked about that shelter and was glad to leave.
Robert reported feeling more positive about the hotel where his
family was subsequently sent. He said, "It was the fun. We go to
the beaches and have picnics. And for Christmas they gave us
presents." He said he felt sad when they left, "cause it was fun
there." Robert is most positive about the current shelter. He said,
"It's more fun here cause this ain't no little room here and we got
enough rooms for me to sleep." He also liked that "they have
movies in the community room."

Robert has been in three different schools for third grade. He said:

> We always be transferring to other schools.
> Everytime you be in a school you have best friends
> and then when you move to a other school you
> miss the friends you had in the old school.

According to his mother, Robert has always done very well in school. He will be promoted to fourth grade next year. Robert seems to be a serious student. He likes "math, art work and reading." He said, "I don't like to play in the classroom. I do my work." When other children try to play with him during class he said that he ignores them.

Like his brother John, Robert spends most of his time after school and on weekends playing baseball and basketball with friends at the park near the shelter. However, he feels that he's "not that good" at sports. He is more confident of his abilities in reading and said he likes to read "any kind of books." Robert said that when he grows up he wants to go to college.

Robert seemed to be somewhat anxious. He said he sometimes has trouble falling asleep at night because he thinks the shadows are monsters. He also said that he sometimes wakes up crying "because I think everybody went somewhere."

INTRODUCTION TO THE PEREZ FAMILY

The Perez family consists of Maria and her three children, Annie age 11, Elizabeth age 10, and Michael age 4. Maria often refers to her son's father, Bobby, as her husband although they are not legally married. Bobby frequently stays with the family, but he cannot legally live at the shelter because he is not entered on Maria's welfare budget.

Maria and her children had lived with Maria's mother in a large apartment. But, when her mother decided to return to Puerto Rico, Maria was unable to pay the rent. They have been in the shelter system for approximately three years, longer than any other family interviewed for this study.

The Perez family lives in a clean and comfortable one bedroom apartment. The two girls sleep in the bedroom. Michael sleeps in the living room with his mother unless his father visits. The family has a television with a Nintendo set in the living room. The children have many toys and two kittens as pets.

Maria, Annie and Elizabeth were interviewed for this study. Interviews took place in either the living room or bedroom of their apartment. All three interviews were arranged for one day, one right after the other. Each first interview lasted approximately 45 minutes. Follow up interviews were conducted several weeks later and were shorter.

Profile of Maria Perez

Maria as a participant in the study. Maria is a thirty year old, overweight woman of Puerto Rican descent. Maria grew up in New York City in a large family of twelve sisters. Most of Maria's family still lives in the Bronx and she visits them frequently. Her parents are now separated. Maria completed eleventh grade but never finished high school. She has never worked.

Maria was among the first women to return her interest form and eagerly signed up to participate in the study when she was contacted. Maria's eagerness was also reflected in the warm manner in which she welcomed me into her home, her offers of food and drink, and her concern for my safety.

In general, Maria discussed her experience in an open and candid way. Still, she appeared somewhat anxious as we began to talk and she smoked cigarettes throughout the interview. There were also times when she seemed hesitant to reveal certain information. For example, she was reluctant to mention Bobby because his presence is against shelter rules. Also, she became anxious when she told me that she occasionally leaves her children alone when she does errands. When reassured about the confidentiality of all information she seemed relieved. When I returned for the second interview she thanked me for talking to her daughters who she thought felt better after talking to me the first time. She said that it was very good for all of them to talk about their experience rather than "keeping everything inside."

Maria's experience. Maria had always lived with her parents and when her mother moved to Puerto Rico she was faced with the insecurity of living without them. She said:

> Well I was living with my parents. So I really didn't have that much worries. I had my kids but my father and mother used to cook dinner for everybody. Now it's that I'm really on my own for the first time, when I became homeless.

When she lost her apartment, Maria she could have stayed with family, but did not feel comfortable doing so because neither her mother nor any of her sisters has adequate space. Maria entered the shelter system because she wanted her own apartment and felt that was the only way to get one. She described her decision:

> I wrapped what little I can and started on this journey. I just don't want to intrude on my family or my kids to be a bother. So I say I'll do this on my own.
>
> And my father said you don't have to leave, you don't got to go through that. You know, you can stay with your sister, wherever, you got family. You can stay with them. I said no. It's just that my mind was made up. I said no, no, no, let me go. And I just left.

Maria also described the difficulties she encountered when she left:

> That was that. I really — I was homeless. I didn't have no place to stay, that was the main reason. And I knew that we wasn't going to stay in the street and that I was going to stay, with my kids, wherever, nobody could tell me I can't stay there.
>
> At the beginning it was hard, I used to cry a lot. Not knowing where I was going to sleep the next day. But after a while I knew I wasn't going to stay in the street, so I just told myself take it easy. I wasn't going to stay in the street because there are places to go.

But, Maria soon discovered the problems with those "places." She and her family have been in and out of the shelter system approximately ten times. When she was unable to tolerate the conditions in a particular shelter or hotel, Maria moved in with her mother-in-law for a brief time. Maria's mother-in-law let her stay whenever she wanted but she was not comfortable living there. The apartment was crowded, and she felt her children were annoying the family. Each time the family returned to the shelter system they had to start the process from the beginning. Maria cited incidents of violence, stealing and drug activity as playing a primary role in her decision to leave a place. For example, she described her experience at one hotel:

> A lot of killings, like in the hallway. Real bad. To me it wasn't that bad because I used to stay indoors. But for the kids, when they used to come from school, they used to see all the transactions in the elevators. Real ugly. And that to me was the worst.

Maria has never been married, but has had two long-term relationships with men, the fathers of her children. Maria has been involved with her son's father, Bobby, for about six years. She described him as her "best friend." Bobby is a construction worker without a steady income. When he does work, he shares his money with Maria. Maria is reluctant to become dependent on him because of the inconsistency of his financial situation. She described her relationship with him:

> I'm not planning to get married. I don't want that at all. But he's always talking about it. He's good. He's real good with the kids. He's real strict with his son. And Annie, she respects him a little but Elizabeth calls him daddy. But me and him, he's wonderful with me. You know, sometimes he works, sometimes he don't work. But he's good, you know. Our relationship is good.

Bobby lives with his mother, but he has been with Maria throughout her homeless experience. She stated:

> Every place I go, even if there's no visitors, he gets in. You know, he gets in legal like not that he runs behind doors. He talks to security, look, you know, please, that's my wife and my kids. And they need somebody to be with them. And security's saying go and they let him up. And he's always been with me through everything. My family loves him. They say, "Maria ain't alone. She got Bobby."

Maria was involved with her daughters' father, Juan, until about seven years ago. She described their relationship as an abusive one. "He was demanding. He used to not let me go out. He used to beat me." She said they broke up "because he's crazy." Juan is currently in jail for selling drugs. Maria continues to keep in touch with Juan's mother for her daughters' sake and allows them to visit their grandmother.

Although Maria has some awareness of the impact of homelessness on her children, she initially denied its effects on her four-year old son:

> He doesn't know nothing. And a lot of times when I had left, he stays with his grandmother, so he don't know. He just gets used to it because it happened so many times.

But, she did say:

> He used to ask about his friends and the other place or his toys. Or when are we going home? Because that was already home for him. And then I said no more. Then he looked at me like, well, like he can't understand it. But every time that happened, it used to disturb him or something. He said, "what are we doing here. Where's our home?"

Maria is more openly worried more about her daughters who are older.

> When I think of how my kids feel, leaving their best doll behind. Because like the time I left Staten Island, they were still in school. And I called my worker and she said, we're going to put you in another hotel. So I just grabbed everything that I could. And that wasn't much at all. So I grabbed the Barbie and left all the others. And that wasn't they favorite one. And when they were looking in the bag, they said, "where's my sneakers or my boots?" Everything was missing. So they suffered and that made me suffer.

Maria is particularly concerned about the impact of homelessness on her daughters' education. She stated:

> When they were in one shelter, they went to a good school. They loved it. And before they knew it, they had to come over here. And they were real depressed. Like why couldn't we still go to that same school. It's all right that we moved but let's just stay in the same school. . . My daughters are left back and everything. Annie's in fourth. She belongs in six. Elizabeth's in third. She belongs in fifth. And it all has to do with being homeless. And I know they're not that smart but they're not stupid at all. . . Just being homeless has been most difficult. And oh, it's a terrible feeling especially when you got children. It's like you're treated different because you're homeless.

Maria is preparing herself for the future. She is beginning to work on her high school equivalency with a teacher at the shelter. She would like to go to school and "take up computers." She also has a job teaching people how to work the laundry at the shelter. She is conflicted about working in the future. "I'd like to get off welfare and work. But first get my apartment. And I've got to raise them up. And I don't want to be a working mother neither. Because of all the neglect I had gave them by the homelessness."

Profile of Elizabeth Perez

Elizabeth as a participant in the study. Elizabeth, a pretty ten year old Hispanic girl, was my first introduction to the Perez family. When I knocked on the door, she opened it a crack and asked what I wanted. A second later she ran out from behind the door promising to take me to her mother. She raced down the stairs ahead of me and motioned for me to follow her outside the building. She called out to her mother who was out in front of the building having just returned from the supermarket. She seemed frightened and had run out without her coat though it was the middle of winter.

I interviewed Elizabeth in her bedroom while the rest of the family spent time in the living room. She seemed very anxious throughout the interview. She seemed to have difficulty staying with a topic and moved quickly from one topic to another. She seemed somewhat wary and suspicious of me during the interview, perhaps because as I later learned, she suspected I was a foster care worker.

Elizabeth's experience.   Elizabeth said she had little understanding of why they left their old apartment and seemed confused when asked. She said, "I don't know why we left." When asked to guess she added:

> Because, you know, too many people. Every time you used to go in the hallway, there used to be a lot of people fighting and smoking crack. In the hallways. That was in the Bronx . . . And then my mother moved to a shelter to get a house. She went and applied. So she came over here . . .And then my mother didn't like it over there so she said she wanted to move. Then she talked to this man or this lady, I don't know who, and they said that she could go in the shelter and she could get herself a house. That's what happened.

Although her understanding of the family's predicament was somewhat limited, Elizabeth expressed strong feelings of fear, guilt, and anger. She described how frightening it was for her to move from place to place:

> Because we used to take trains with a lot of bags. So then my father, you know, he used to help us. He used to carry all the bags. And I wouldn't like the trains, they're scary. Because I heard a lot of people got hurt falling into the tracks. And I didn't like it because my father be, you know, just walking there to hold the pole. And I'd be scared. I'd be saying to my brother come over here. And I'd be scared. And my mother says, he's okay. I might be standing next to him so he don't fall, God forbid.

Elizabeth shared many of her fears during the interview. For example, she said:

Some people be taking kids around here. Once I heard in the news that a kid got chopped up. And I was scared and I used to have nightmares. And I used to go sleep with my mother. I heard on the news that a girl, she looked through the peek hole and a man shot the peek hole and she got shot in the eye. That's why I don't like looking through the peek hole. I just say, "Who?" I know my mother's knock. My mother knocks like that . . .Sometimes I feel bad that my mother be reading newspapers to us, bad things that a girl got raped. She reads it to us that we could be careful in the streets.

Elizabeth suggested that she felt responsible for at least one move the family made. In her description of an incident that occurred while the family was staying with her brother's grandmother, she seemed to feel that both the fight and the resulting move were her fault. She said:

Once there was a big fight between my mother and my stepfather's sister. My father was on my mother's side. My father was hitting his own sister. It was a big fight and I was crying. Because you know my mother was screaming and my father went to jail. They put him in the police car and he came back. It was about my father's sister was talking about that she don't like me. They were just talking about it in the kitchen and my mother heard her and she got mad. And when they came outside there was a big fight in front of the building.

Elizabeth said that she did not like the big barracks shelters and appeared to be angry at the conditions to which she was subjected:

Well, I used to not like it because they used to feed you food. They used to make you eat. You got to go to a little cafeteria and everybody eats. They used to give nasty food. They give breakfast, lunch and dinner. If you don't wake up early, you can't eat. Then you be starved. They won't let you out, only sometimes, you know, you got to write your name when you're going to go out on the

paper. And they'll know who's out or in. And if
you come in late, real late, the doors are closed
and you be locked out. And they'll throw your
things out and you won't be in the shelter no more.

Elizabeth is currently in third grade at a public school around
the corner from the shelter. She has been left back twice and
should be in fifth grade. She feels her school difficulty acutely,
"That's why I don't hardly know how to read because I've been
missing school too much." She reported that she is well behaved in
school. She said,

> Some kids in my class, sometimes they be bad to
> the teacher. And the teacher goes to call the
> principal and they get a letter sent home. And
> that's why I always be good and I never get a letter
> sent.

Elizabeth is very sensitive about fighting. She rated the many
different schools she attended in terms of how much fighting went
on. For example, when asked about her current school she said,
"It's better than the other ones because the other ones, they used to
be too much fights. And over here, they ain't have much fights.
And it's okay over here."
Elizabeth says she likes her current school, and she would like
to stay. She expresses this wish with the fantasy that her family
will get an apartment near the school. She said:

> Now we're staying here to get a house. And we've
> been in so many shelters and they haven't given us
> a house. So my mother said that she's going to
> come here. And after this, she'll get a project
> house. I'm going to still go to that school.
> Because when we get a project, it's around here.

> In her journey from place to place, there have been
> other schools that she has liked and had a hard
> time leaving. For example, when asked how she
> felt about leaving one such school after seven
> months she stated:

> I felt sad. I mean I started crying to my mother. I
> said, "Ma, I don't want to leave this school." She

says, "Well, we have to because we're moving."
And then we moved and we came to another
shelter. Then we got here.

Elizabeth has two good friends, one who lives in the shelter and
another one who is in her class. Elizabeth sees both friends after
school. She goes to the library with her friend from school. They do
their homework there. She said, "I go upstairs to my friend on the
fifth floor and we play. And then we make up work and we work.
We make ourselves laugh. And we make stories." When she is not
in school Elizabeth described that she plays with her friends, cleans
the house or reads. She said, "I clean up the house or I lay down
and read a book. Because I got a library there." Elizabeth likes to
read and is proud that she can take books from the library. She
showed me her library card and the books she had taken out.

Elizabeth reported that she helps her mother as much as she
can. She does whatever household chores are required. She said, "I
like to clean up my room. Pick up all my belongings. Because it's
not nice to leave the things all around. And it's nice to keep it
where your things are at and put them away."

Elizabeth feels her mother has helped her through the
experience and has been supportive when she needed her most. She
seems very close to her mother.

> We used to be in a van, she used to say, if you're
> tired or hungry we'll stop in the store. She used to
> stop in the store and she used to buy us cheese. Or
> a little sweet that is made already and cheese.
> And we used to lay on her lap and we used to go to
> sleep. Then when we there, she used to say, girls
> we're there. And we used to go upstairs and we
> used to just go to sleep and when we wake up in
> the morning fix everything. And put all the clothes
> in the drawers.

Elizabeth also feels that her sister helps her.

> When my mother goes out to the store. My sister
> used to say, 'Come on Michael and Elizabeth.'
> She used to bring us in the back of the apartment
> and we all play around not to be scared. Because
> we used to be scared when my mother goes out.

Profile of Annie Perez

Annie as a participant in the study. Annie is an attractive 11 year old girl. She was interviewed in the bedroom she shares with her sister. She appeared nervous throughout the interview and was able to verbalize her feelings:

> Okay, I'm dying to get this finished. Because like
> I feel so scared. I feel like nervous. I don't know.
> You know, because it's hard to talk to somebody
> about my feelings. Because, you know, it's hard to
> let them out. There's so much.

Annie blinked her eyes frequently, talked quickly and changed topics often throughout the interview.

Annie's experience. When asked how she became homeless, Annie said:

> My mother didn't like it where we lived in the
> Bronx anymore. There was too much drugs
> outside, too many people smoking crack. So we
> went to stay with my aunt but there wasn't room.
> We all slept in one bed. So my mother called to
> see about getting a house and they told her come
> to the shelter and we'll find you a house. So we
> went to the shelter and we still don't have a house.

Annie described her feelings each time the family moved to another shelter or hotel:

> When I used to get there, I used to be scared
> because the school, I didn't know how it was going
> to be, how it was going to turn out, how was the
> next thing going to be, you know. I be scared of
> the next day, how is it going to turn out. And, you
> know, sometimes I be scared, I be like, oh, God,
> please let something good happen. Because I don't
> know what's coming up the next day, if they gonna
> hurt us, something like that, because I be scared.
> Things like that. But now, like I'm used to it, you
> know.

Annie said that she liked it at some big shelters because she met many people:

> It was warm. Because I was used to everybody. Everybody in there was my friend. You know, it's fun because, you know, it feels like, you know, so exciting. And my mother has a lot of friends. There are no fights.

Annie often thinks about the ordeal she has been through.

> Well, it stays in my head. See, sometimes when I'm bored, it's like . . . just sitting there like this and it just pops up in my head. And then I just stare at the wall thinking about all those things. What's going to happen next. Like my conscience tells me, what's going to happen next? I start thinking about it a lot and I got to go and get it out of my head. . . Sometimes, I have a lot of bad dreams.

Annie worries that her brother and sister will blame her mother for going through this experience. She said:

> Like about my brother. Like I wonder what's going to happen when he get big, how he's going to feel about this, how he's going to feel about my mother, you know, what we're going through. And my sister, like if my sister's going to think like it's my mother's fault, you know, something like that.

Annie talked about issues of responsibility throughout her interview. She worries about money. She would like to work so she could earn money for her family and for herself. She thinks she could buy a house if she worked. She said:

> I'm looking forward to being twelve. Trying to be thirteen so I could work in MacDonald's. They told me if I wanted a job. And twelve and then thirteen and then I can work. Because I like to work. Make a lot of money. Buy clothes. Get a house. I'm trying to get a house. Because it's fun to be, you know, like in a house. And you feel safe. And

you don't have to be around people so much. To
be by myself in the family. Because I'm a girl that
likes to stay in the house. I don't go out so much.
I don't like it. I don't like the streets. I like to be
in my house with my family.

Both Annie and her sister receive an allowance if they do certain
household chores. According to her mother, Annie saves her money.
She gives her mother money when she runs out.

Although Annie is only one year older than her sister she
watches her brother and sister when her mother goes out. She said:

Like when my mother goes next door, I keep a
good eye on them because I don't want nothing to
happen to my brother. And they listen to me when
I tell them. I watch them. Because I take good
care of them. I don't leave them next to the stove.
And I cook. I know how to cook. I know how to
make a lot of things. I know how to make eggs,
rice, beans, chicken and a lot of things. I help my
mother with the food. I make cakes on holidays.

Annie is in fourth grade but should be in sixth. She explains
her difficulty in terms of moving around so much. She said:

It was hard moving to so many schools. That was
hard. Because I used to leave there and then I
probably miss the test and I had to go to another
one and catch up with them. Catch up, that was
hard, too. I'm supposed to be in the sixth going
into seventh. So many schools I had to switch. I
didn't know what was next so I missed a lot of
things.

Annie stated that she tries to behave appropriately in school.
She said, "I'm not so smart but, you know, I try the best I can. You
know, I'm not dumb but I'm, you know, I'm good." But, her mother
reports that according to her teacher she spends too much time
fooling around with her best friend who is in the same class. Annie
also gets into fights if she is provoked by the other children.

The hardest thing for Annie was the uncertainty about what was
going to happen next:

> And it was hard, you know, it was real hard
> because we didn't know what was next. You don't
> even know if you're going to die the next day. I
> don't even know if I'm going to die tomorrow, God
> forbid, you know. So that's the hard part.

Annie feels she gets much support from her mother and siblings.
When she needs to talk about her experience she goes to her
mother.

> My mother helps me when things are hard. She be
> with me all the way. You know, she never left me.
> You know, she be there all through everything
> when I needed her, when I needed to cry over my
> things. I needed somebody to lean on and I had
> my mother there to lean on. My sister, my brother.
> You know, it was always us four. Me and my
> sister and my brother and my mother, it was
> always us four that hanged on to each other.

Annie prays that her situation will improve. She hopes for an
apartment.

> And I pray almost every day but not every day.
> Sometimes I forget. But God forgives me, you
> know, for forgetting. Because sometimes when I
> go to the movie, I fall asleep and I forget to pray.
> So that happens and then God forgives me. He
> knows that I really meant to pray. And God helps
> me, too. All I got to — let's say if I'm sick, I just
> run to God and he'll make me feel better. Like I
> always say, God, please let me have my apartment
> — like where we are now, just to the tip of the
> apartment, right there. Just right around the corner.

Annie feels sad about losing things. She tries to keep her
Christmas gifts together in one bag, "I put my things in the bag and
if I move, I always have my things ready." She explained:

> I don't like to lose things. I lost a lot. Like, you
> know, clothes. Like dresses. No, like — little
> bitty things like one   doll. But one doll is a lot
> to me. Because when somebody gives me even

like a powder, it's a lot for me, you know, because
I'm like sensitive. And anything they give me, I
appreciate.

Annie spends most of her time in the shelter either in her own
apartment or her friend's apartment. She said that she often helps
her mother with housework but her mother disagrees. She stated
that Annie will not do anything unless she really keeps after her.
Annie said:

And I don't go outside often. I don't go out at all. I
don't even remember times when I go. I clean the
house. I play Nintendo. I study my words. I got
some spelling words. I study my words, I keep my
house clean, take care of, you know, take care of
my things.

Annie likes to jump rope. She is proud of her skill. She said:

I'm in the double dutch contest and the other — in
the end of the year, I get to do the contests, school
by school, city by city . . . And I be first and the
fastest.

Annie has a best friend in the shelter who is very important to
her. Her mother says that she finds a best friend wherever they go.
Annie anticipates feeling very sad when she moves and has to leave
her friend.   She expressed the wish that they will always stay
together and described that they will live together when they get an
apartment:

My best friend is upstairs. I've been with her for
five years. We were together. And we went
through a lot together. We went through one
shelter together. We went to camp together and
we're still here. You know, for five years we been
friends. Because like if I was to leave, I'll cry.

INTRODUCTION TO THE GARCIA FAMILY

The Garcia family consists of Linda and her two children, Jimmy, age 11, and Erica, age 3. They have been in the shelter system for approximately eleven months. The Garcia family lives in a cramped, yet clean, one bedroom apartment. There were two beds in each room. The children sleep in the bedroom while Linda sleeps in the living room. There was also a small table with a black and white television and several chairs in the living area. Some of Erica's toys such as a small desk with chalkboard were scattered around the apartment. Jimmy kept his toys and games stored neatly in a dresser in the bedroom.

Linda and Jimmy were interviewed for this study. Interviews took place in their apartment at the shelter, usually in the living room. Linda and her son were interviewed twice. Each interview with Linda lasted close to one hour while Jimmy's interviews were approximately thirty minutes long. Second interviews were conducted for clarification and additional information several weeks after the first interviews.

Profile of Linda Garcia

Linda as a participant in the study. Linda is a thirty-three year old woman of Hispanic descent. Linda was born into a large family and she was raised in New York City. She is bilingual, speaking both Spanish and English. She walks with a slight limp due to arthritis. Linda dropped out of high school in eleventh grade, but returned for her GED. She trained to be a secretary and did work for a few years before her son was born.

Linda eagerly agreed to participate in the study. She greeted me warmly when she was contacted and kept all scheduled appointments. Linda and I quickly developed a close rapport. During the interview, she shared information freely, seemed to relax, and to enjoy talking about her experience. She kissed me goodbye after the second interview and invited me to come visit her in her new apartment.

Linda's experience. Linda lived in Puerto Rico until eleven months ago. She had moved there five years prior after separating from her son's father. She said that she left because she discovered that he was using cocaine. She said, "It was something I had to do.

I'm not going to jeopardize my children's health or my income for drugs." She originally went to Puerto Rico on vacation but liked it so much she decided to stay. While there she married a man she met at church and had a daughter, Erica. When her husband became abusive she decided to leave him and return to New York.

> I left Puerto Rico because I was having some problems with my husband. We got legally married but he has an alcohol problem which I tried to take care of. But it got to the point he got violent because he had a fall. He fractured his head. That resulted in him getting seizures all of the time. And emotionally it was affecting me. It was affecting the kids. And I thought that if it got to the point the neighbors got involved, I would actually lose my kids. Because sometimes they will do that. If they see that, well, you don't decide to get out of the house and he gets violent, then it's going to affect your children. We will have to take them away from you. I wasn't going to lose my kids on his account. So I thought it was the best thing to do. Start a new life and get them away from all that tension.

Thus, Linda decided to leave a potentially dangerous situation. Her initial plan was to stay with her sister until she could find a place of her own. Financial difficulties and overcrowded conditions interfered with this plan. Linda explained:

> It really didn't work out because she had three kids. She had just had her case closed by welfare for some reason. And economically-wise, you know, there was no way for me to get any money or anything unless I went out on my own.

Linda's feelings of frustration as well as concern for her sister prompted her to leave.

> I couldn't take it. You know, it was very difficult to see that there was no way I could have any means of support for her or me. She had her own husband and kids, so I didn't want to be a burden to them. She had three of her own plus my two. So it

was five kids running all over the house, and no
place to go. And she's sick. She has a bit of
asthma and stuff. So I didn't want to be no trouble.
I said if I did it before, I took care of them on my
own before and really didn't have a bad time, I can
do it again.

After leaving her sister's apartment, Linda went with her
children to the Emergency Assistance Unit and entered the shelter
system. Because the whole family was sick, they were not placed
in a large barracks shelter, typically the first stop in the system.
Linda explained:

They did send me to a shelter in the Bronx but
when I got there, the doctor checked us out. He
said it wasn't a good idea to be in such a crowded
area being that we were all sick. . . I could have
actually spread my cold around and gotten
everybody else sick. They decided to send me
back to EAU until I got into a hotel.

Linda recalled that she worried constantly while she lived in
the hotel:

When I was in the hotel I didn't know what would
happen. I used to worry about everything. Where
my food was coming from, where my kids were
going to be staying, schooling, everything. I would
get depressed enough. I would go lock myself in
my room and cry. But then I would say, well,
there's got to be somebody I can talk to, some way
I can do something, and I started moving. I started
going places.

She said that she had trouble sleeping in the hotel because she was
so concerned about her family's safety:

I couldn't sleep very well because everybody
would be running up and down. You would wonder
was the door safe enough? Would someone come
in? Would there be any arguments? Would my
children be safe enough?

Since the bathroom was not in the room, she said that she could not go to the toilet or shower without worrying about leaving her children alone in the room:

> The first day they actually tried to kick the door down because I guess somebody saw that I was in the shower. And they tried kicking the door to get inside. And my kids started screaming.

In contrast, Linda had nothing but praise for her current placement.

> It's been great here. You know, if I have to choose between being in the shelter or a hotel, or being here, I would recommend to be put here. It's very nice. There's a lot of security. There's a lot of people helping out. We have social workers here nine to five. We have guards during the night in case of any emergency.

She described her first impression.

> The first day I came in I thought maybe it's just one little room. And you're not going to feel comfortable. You're going to be out of place. But everybody treated me so nicely when I came in. And when I came and saw it was an actual apartment and they would be more comfortable, they would sleep better. They wouldn't have problems with anybody trying to get in, anybody trying to bother them. I said, this is great.

Linda expressed great concern about her children. She feels the experience has been very difficult for her son. She observed he was depressed when he first came to New York from Puerto Rico. She said:

> Jimmy was depressed because he didn't like the idea of switching around so often. And all of a sudden, he has to start a new school, new friends, new house, new everything. And I can understand that. I didn't like to have to be moving around. When we lived in the hotel he wouldn't want to do

some of the work. Like I used to get complaints from the teacher in May that he would sit in the classroom but really wouldn't want to work. But things cleared up, you know, after a while. And we talked. I talked to the principal. I talked to the teachers. I told the teacher, you have to understand Jimmy is no longer with his father. We were away for so long he has to get used to using the English language a lot. You know, most of the kids in here are not bilingual so he can't really talk to them. He is a shy person because my son even with me, sometimes he's so shy I can't get him to say things I want him to say.

Linda said that she is very pleased with the way her three year old daughter, Erica, has adjusted to the many changes in her life since they moved from Puerto Rico. She has picked up the English language very quickly. She attends preschool at the shelter and her teachers have told Linda that she is very bright and doing well there. Linda was initially worried about Erica's adjustment and watches her for signs of difficulty. She said,

When I separated from her father in February, I thought emotionally she was going to have a hard time. But I guess since she was little at the time when we left, she actually doesn't ask for him. It's like it really didn't affect her as much as I thought it would. She's very cautious about me going in and out and being away for a couple of minutes or an hour or so. So I know there's something behind that. She's not emotionally saying anything because she's still a baby. But she might be thinking, maybe Daddy disappears so maybe Mommy will disappear. She'll go downstairs and may not come back. I don't want her to go out on me too.

Linda said that she talks openly with her children and tries to explain everything that happens. She said, "I don't believe in having secrets from my kids." Regarding her son she added,

I talk to him all the time. If I see something's worrying him, I tell him, well, you know you can

talk to me. If it's your fault, we'll try to find out
why it happened. And if it isn't your fault, we'll try
to find out, you know, who's at fault. Why are you
like this? Why are you feeling that way?

Linda is currently involved with a man she dated briefly before
she went to Puerto Rico. She says that she is happy with the
relationship but is cautious about getting overly involved right now.
She stated,

> Our relationship's been fine. It was over six years
> that I hadn't seen him. But things are working out.
> He's trying his best. Right now he's without a job.
> He's very helpful. And the kids love him,
> especially my daughter. She calls him daddy.
> They have a very good relationship. I just hope it
> will keep that way and there won't be any changes
> that she'll be hurt emotionally. We're not really
> ready to just rush into anything and have
> something happen and get hurt.

Linda's mother and stepfather still live in Puerto Rico. She
described that she relied on them in Puerto Rico but has turned to
other relatives for support since returning to New York. Besides her
sister who she initially stayed with, she is reestablishing contact
with other relatives. She said:

> Last week I went and visited a sister of mine I
> hadn't seen since I left for Puerto Rico. I spent the
> night with her. From there I went to my Dad, spent
> all day with him. And I got in touch with them.
> It was really nice. We had a nice time. After
> being away so long you want to know all the good
> things that happened. And I found out one of my
> sister's had gotten married while I was away. The
> other one's expecting a baby. And my Dad's got a
> nice job now.

Linda has a part time job at the shelter running the toy library
through which parents can borrow toys for their children. She earns
some money from this job. Although she enjoys the job she said
that she does not want to work full-time in the future because she
feels her children would suffer. She said:

> I don't think at this time I would want to go to work
> until they are able to take care of themselves. And
> in the meantime, no. I mean, I may work like right
> now, a part-time job. And I know I'll be home at
> certain hour. But I wouldn't want to work all the
> time and really not be there.

Linda dropped out of school in eleventh grade but returned for her GED. She trained to be a secretary and did work for a few years before she had her son.

Profile of Jimmy Garcia

Jimmy as a participant in the study. Jimmy is a handsome but overweight eleven year old boy. He was interviewed in the bedroom he shares with his sister. Jimmy appeared anxious and was reticent throughout the interview. Spanish is his first language, and he spoke English haltingly and with an accent. He frequently said, "I don't know," in response to questions. He often provided brief answers to questions, and it took much questioning for him to elaborate on his response. He told his story more easily when asked to draw pictures to help describe the different places he stayed.

Jimmy's experience. Jimmy has a clear understanding that it was his stepfather's abusive behavior that resulted in his family's move to New York City. He said:

> Because — (long pause) — because my sister's
> father was hitting my mother too much and she
> left. Every day and every day when he got drunk,
> every time he was hitting my mother. And one
> time, I almost hit him with my bat like that.

Jimmy described what it was like to live with his aunt during their early days in New York:

> It was not so good living with my aunt because she
> had her husband — her husband was from Santo
> Domingo. And he was bad. Any time the kids
> didn't do whatever he said, he smack them and
> everything. He was really bad. And every time he

would take money from my aunt, from her purse,
because she was sleeping.

When they left his aunt's house and moved into the hotel,
Jimmy quickly made friends with another boy there. He said:

I used to play with my neighbor friend. We used to
play with a little machine, like a television but
little like that. We used to go sometimes to a park
at 24th street. We went on the slides and playing
tag. He move to Queens after we left.

Jimmy said that he was not afraid while living in the hotel but
he knew many children who were. He said:

They used to say a monster came at six o'clock. A
lot of the kids used to say it but I used to stay
outside until seven and there wasn't no monster. I
used to sit on the stairs and there wasn't nothing.

Jimmy described problems with some children at the hotel:

They were causing trouble. They were bad kids.
They used to pick on little kids and everything.
Sometimes they pick on me. One time they did. I
was fighting with one. They were stepping on my
shoes that my mother bought me. Then I started
fighting with them.

Jimmy said that he likes living in the shelter. He seems to feel
safe when he plays outside because:

They got a camera in front. So they could see that
they don't do nothing bad in the courtyard. They
can see through there everybody. If they see
something, they go running out of the office and
get them and take them to the office until their
mother come.

He described that he has made many friends and plays outside with
them whenever he can. He said:

> When it snows we go play fight in the snow or we
> go in the park of our school yard. And sometimes
> we go to the park over there to play baseball.
> That's my bat. I like football too. Sometimes I go
> from the morning to the afternoon.

Jimmy is one year behind where he should be in school. His
mother chose to have him repeat first grade when they moved to
Puerto Rico. According to his mother he is doing well in fifth grade
now. He is placed in an ESL class that has really made a
difference. She said that he had always been a good student but his
grades began to slip after they moved to New York. He was
switched to three schools very quickly. He attended one school for
a month while they stayed at his aunt's house, another for three
months while they lived in the hotel and is now in his third school
near the shelter. He recalled the school he attended while he lived
in the hotel:

> It was good. My teacher was good too. And over
> there the homework, it was easy, like
> multiplication, division but easy. Not like over
> here. And the school yard was bigger than that one
> and they had two yards, one inside and one
> outside. And it had swings and everything. I felt
> sad when I left there. Only once I got to go on a
> trip over there.

At times, Jimmy says he feels picked on by his teacher in the
school he goes to now. He feels he is often wrongly accused of
starting trouble. However, he says that he has many friends in
school and likes to play with them during recess. He said, "Almost
the whole class are my friends. And from other classes. I got about
ten more."

Jimmy said that he misses his friends in Puerto Rico very much.
He speaks fondly of them,

> I used to go with my friends playing in the park
> around in back of my house. There was a door to
> go. And I used to go every time. We played
> basketball and frisbee. The hardest thing was
> when I left. Because all of my friends, they were
> telling me to don't leave. I lived there four years.

He said that he had a best friend named Roberto. "He used to come and we would play. I still got two cards that he gave me." Jimmy has held onto those cards throughout his journey.

Jimmy would like to be a firefighter when he grows up. At the shelter he says that he likes to go outside and play baseball with his friends. He also likes to watch cartoons on television. He said that he watches his sister when his mother needs to run an errand or sometimes when she works at her job at the shelter. While I was there he eagerly picked his sister up from school and brought her home.

INTRODUCTION TO THE SMITH FAMILY

The Smith family consists of Evelyn and her two daughters, Dana age 12, and Cindy age 6. Evelyn's boyfriend, John, also stays with them. Evelyn also has an 18 year old son who has lived with one of his uncles for the past four years. They have been in the shelter system for approximately sixteen months and in the current shelter for eight months.

The Smith family lives in one-bedroom apartment at the shelter. Unwashed dishes piled high in the kitchen and dirty sheets in the bedroom contributed to the generally ill-kept appearance of the apartment. Evelyn sleeps in the living room with John while her daughters share the bedroom. They have a cat who Dana says they got to catch the mice which reportedly frequently run through the apartment. While I was there the television was always on. They were the only family I met in the shelter who had a telephone that Evelyn was able to get since her daughter, Cindy, has asthma.

Evelyn and Dana's interviews took place in the living room while Cindy was interviewed in her bedroom. Evelyn and Dana were interviewed twice. Cindy refused a second interview. First interviews lasted forty-five minutes. Second interviews were shorter and served to clarify information obtained in the first session.

Profile of Evelyn Smith

Evelyn as a participant in the study. Evelyn is a 35 year old Black woman who is a diabetic. She grew up in a large family in the southern United States. Evelyn came to New York at the age of eighteen to live with one of her sisters. Only after several attempts did I find her at home. She was in the hall watching several small children for a neighbor who had gone to the supermarket.

Evelyn appeared to be quite eager to participate in the study. During the interview, she talked openly about her experience. She was angry about how she was treated and seemed glad to have somebody listen to her. She fell asleep while I interviewed her daughter.

Evelyn's experience. Evelyn and her children lived in what she described as a dilapidated apartment in Brooklyn. Evelyn had taken her landlady to court in an effort to compel her to make necessary repairs. However, the family was evicted before the city arranged for an inspection. She explained:

> I just got put out of my apartment. The landlord told me she wanted the apartment for her family. But she didn't want it for her family. She rented it out to somebody else.

Evelyn feels she was evicted from her apartment because the landlady did not like her family, but she does not know why they were not liked. After the eviction, Evelyn lived with her extended family for a short time before entering the shelter system. First, they moved in with her brother. However, Evelyn and her children found it very uncomfortable at her brother's house. She said:

> Me and my brother can't get along. . . I didn't like it there because he had us down in the basement. And the room that we were sleeping in, we ain't got no air because he had painted over the windows. We was all sleeping in one room. And he had a lot of junk and stuff down there. And he had mice and things, rats running around down there. And different kinds of spiders. And then one day, the boiler caught on fire. I was taking them to the bathroom and the boiler down there caught on fire. . . I couldn't take it there. . . He put me out.

After being asked to leave her brother's house Evelyn's family stayed with her younger daughter's grandmother. Although Evelyn is no longer involved with this woman's son, the grandmother allowed them to sleep on the floor in her house. However, Evelyn soon began having difficulties there. Tension arose when her host noticed some money missing. Evelyn explained:

> It wasn't her fault but me and her don't get along. . .
> She thought I was taking her money. But I told her
> son took it. Because he had put the blame on me.
> Why should I take her money when I had my own
> money? And he was taking his mother's money.

After being asked to leave that household, Evelyn went to a
friend's house, but the friend had no room for them. Thus, Evelyn
and her family entered the shelter system. She describes her
introduction to this system:

> My friend and her father took us to the precinct
> and they called the Emergence Assistance Unit for
> us, and the cops put us on the train because we
> didn't have no money to get on the train, and we
> went there. And they had a place, they sent us to a
> hotel. And by the time we got there, they had
> called and canceled. So we had to go all the way
> back there again. They were sending us from
> shelter to shelter. We literally could only stay for
> one night. And I got tired of staying for one night.
> So I just got tired of running from shelter to shelter
> so I went back to my welfare center.

Eventually, Evelyn and her children were placed in a hotel
where they were able to stay for a longer time. However, she
disliked the hotel because she found it to be dangerous. She said:

> When I first went there, I was kind of scared. Most
> of them was on drugs so I just stayed in my room.
> So then, a couple nights, kids from the hotel next
> door would come in there. They took the garbage
> cans in, close the people's doors and set them on
> fire. So the next day I talked to my crisis worker
> and told her I couldn't take it no more.

Although she said she was unhappy with the hotel, Evelyn was
quite selective about where she would accept a placement. She
turned down a few placements because they were too far away.
Finally, her crisis worker allowed her to look at the book of
placements and told her to choose any place she wanted. She
chose the current shelter because of its proximity to her daughters'
schools.

Evelyn said she is not satisfied with her current placement either. She feels that other women in the shelter make up stories about her and try to get her in trouble with the shelter staff. She gave an example:

> This girl she go and take it to the front that I drew
> a knife on her. And I asked her where is the knife.
> And I don't have a knife in my hand. Because she
> had started the mess. Then we all went down for a
> meeting with a worker because she took it to the
> front office.

Evelyn feels the worker she has at the shelter is not on her side when these incidents occur.

Evelyn likes to get away from the shelter on weekends. She has a sister whom she frequently visits. She brings the children and does not return to the shelter until late at night. Her sister helps her and gives them food when they need it. She said:

> Well when we get there, we haven't eaten,
> something like that, she fix dinner stuff, cold stuff
> for us and we eat. Then before we leave she fixes
> us stuff and we brings it home with us. Then when
> I get home I call her to know that we got home
> okay.

Evelyn attends a training program at a vocational school. She is learning to work with computers and studying for her GED. She said that the program requires a substantial commitment of time and energy. She attends school every afternoon from 1:30 to 6:30. She said she spends so much time in school that she has little time to participate in the activities at the shelter. She said she does try to go to some meetings like the self-help group, but has to leave early.

Evelyn's daughter Dana helps her while she's in school by watching her younger daughter. She said:

> When I go to school, she picks up Cindy. And all I
> do is tell them to stay upstairs and don't open the
> door for nobody. Then when I come in, by the time
> I get out of school, she have everything did by the
> time I get there.

Profile of Dana Smith

Dana as a participant in the study. Dana is a pretty 12 year old girl who looks much older than her stated age. She is overweight and appeared to be pregnant. While neither Dana nor her mother mentioned this during their interviews, her pregnancy was later confirmed by staff at the shelter. While she looked very put together during the first visit, during the second she looked disheveled as if she had just woken up even though it was the afternoon.

Dana was interviewed in the living room of their apartment. She is more articulate than her mother and she spoke openly about her experience in the shelter system. However, during the second interview she had little to add and seemed somewhat annoyed at the further questioning.

Dana's experience. Dana's understanding of why they were evicted from their apartment is similar to her mother's. She said, referring to their landlady:

She said she wanted the apartment for her son. And after we moved out she rented one of the rooms, one of the bedrooms out to somebody else.

Dana liked where they lived before but acknowledged many problems. About the neighborhood she stated, "Every where you'd go, you'd always run into a drug problem or something like that" and added about their apartment:

> It was nice. It was just that everything in the house that need to be repaired, the landlord always said that she was going to have it repaired, and she never had it fixed. And during the wintertime, the windows, the sides of the windows needed to be fixed so the cold air wouldn't come in. She said she was going to have new windows put in there. She never did. Until it started getting real, real cold, then that's when she had new windows put in. Because my mother had took her to court, so she didn't have no other choice but to give us new windows.

When the family moved into her uncle's house after being evicted, Dana did not like the accommodations. She and her sister were afraid to use the bathroom. She said:

> And right by the bathroom, the boiler's sitting right there. And, me and my sister would always be scared to go back there because sometimes the boiler would blow off and everything and it would start smoking. So every time we wanted to go to the bathroom, we wouldn't go back there by ourselves unless my mother came back there with us.

However, she had no complaints about her uncle while they stayed there. She said:

> He was okay. He didn't really say too much to me. So I don't have no complaint. He's not so good, but he never said anything or did anything to me.

She doesn't understand why he won't let them get their belongings from his apartment.

> He got all our stuff there. Everything that we took there with us when we moved out of our apartment. He still has that there. He won't let us in the house to get it. Every time we go there, he won't let us in. It's either he act like he ain't home or he come to the door and he tell us to leave because he won't let us in.

Dana felt satisfied when they moved in with her sister's grandmother after leaving her uncle's house. However, traveling to school which was far away was a problem. She had to ride two trains and it "took a long time."

Dana was scared when they moved into the hotel. She said:

> When we first moved there, I wasn't so scared because it was okay. And then once the drugs started coming into there and they started to build fires, started breaking out fires and everything, that's what started to worry me. Because night after night they would ring the fire bell and

> sometimes there's going to be a fire. And if my
> sister would be asleep, she'd jump up out of her
> sleep and starts crying. And it scared her a lot.

Dana is happier with her current living situation. She said,
"We've got it going good here and everything." However, she does
not seem to have friends at the shelter and does not participate in
any activities. For example when asked what she does after school
she said:

> I just come upstairs, clean up what I have to clean.
> Got to do my homework. If I don't go to sleep I
> watch TV. Most likely every afternoon I fall
> asleep because when I get out of school I be tired.

On weekends her schedule is similar.

> If I don't go to my aunt's house I just stay in the
> house. I do nothing, sleep, work. Nothing much. I
> don't deal with the kids around here as much as I
> used to. I don't go outside no more. Not as much
> as I used to. A lot of my friends moved.

The hardest thing for Dana through all the moves they made
was getting to school. She said:

> I had to travel everyday taking two or more trains
> to get to school. I'm not no early bird. my mother
> wake me up 6 o'clock. I'd get up and I'd go back
> to school. So either way, if I'd get up at six and
> leave the house at 6:30. It'd still take me a long
> time to get to school because of the trains. In the
> morning when they start running, they run out slow.
> So it would take me a long time to get to school.
> That was my biggest problem.

Dana is currently placed in a seventh grade special education
class. She has been in special education since third grade because
"sometimes I can't control my temper." She likes some of the
subjects she's studying but does not like "the kids and some of the
teachers. I don't like the kids that much because they like to pick
on me and everything."

Dana has missed a lot of school this year because of a chronic back problem. While I was interviewing the family a truant officer came from the school to investigate her many absences. She had missed twenty days in the first three months of school. Dana said that she has been to see several doctors about her back but none was able to determine what is wrong.

Dana would like to be mainstreamed into a regular education class. However, her many absences interfere with her progress. She said:

> When I get sick that's the only reason I'm not getting out. Because when I'm sick I can't do the work. Because they said if I come in all the time, they'll mainstream me. And after I've been mainstreamed for a couple of months, they'll be able to take me out of special ed and put me in a regular class. But they can't do it because I'm always absent.

Dana feels her education is important and would like to be a lawyer when she grows up. She said, "In school one of my teacher's given me a book studying the law and stuff. So basically, I wanted to be a lawyer."

Throughout her experience with homelessness Dana feels her aunt has been most helpful to her and her family. She said:

> When we had problems we would go to her with them. She would help us out and everything. And some of the nights when we didn't want to come back home, she would let us stay there. She helped us a lot. She looks for apartment for my mother and everything.

Profile of Cindy Smith

Cindy as a participant in the study. Cindy is a pretty, small girl one month short of her sixth birthday. She was initially shy but, with her mother's encouragement, agreed to be interviewed. As she grew more comfortable, Cindy eagerly showed me her dolls and other toys. During the interview, her answers were generally short, and she needed encouragement and questioning in order to. She was better able to describe her experience while drawing pictures. Although Cindy agreed to the first interview, when I returned for the second time she wasn't feeling well and said she did not want to talk again.

Cindy's experience. Cindy had little understanding of why they left their apartment in Brooklyn. She did not know why the landlady told them to leave. Cindy remembered the apartment fondly:

> Me and my sister went outside to play in the snow.
> Or sometimes me and my sister go outside and I
> call my friends from the window and we play rope.

Cindy said that she didn't like it when they moved into her uncle's house. She said:

> We stayed in the basement. They stayed upstairs.
> There was mice and I used to be scared. I didn't
> want to go to the bathroom by myself. There was a
> fire near there. I used to go with my mother and
> my sister.

Cindy knew that most of their belongings are still at her uncle's house but does not seem too bothered by it. She said,

> All the stuff we had before we came here is at my
> uncle's house. I have more clothes than my mother
> and sister because my cousin gave them to me.
> She gave me the clothes that couldn't fit and her
> mother brought her some more.

Regarding the family's next move to her grandmother's house Cindy recalled some conflict with her cousin who was also living there,

> My oldest cousin she used to run through the house
> and get me in trouble. She would get me and my
> other cousin in trouble. We wasn't running through
> the house it was her. When I caught her by herself
> I beat her up.

Cindy remembered moving to many different shelters. She said, "In the first place we didn't have anything to eat. The second place we did. We had cheese and sandwiches." She said that she did not like the first place because she was hungry. She has asthma which she associates to living in the shelters. She said, "I got it when we was living in all those shelters. At night I can't breath because the window was down."

Cindy was adamant about her dislike for the hotel they stayed in for eight months. She said, "I didn't like it. We didn't have no kitchen. My mommy bought a little stove. And all the time there be fires at night. I was scared and fell out of my bed." According to Cindy the family didn't go out much when they lived at the hotel. She said that they mostly stayed in the room and watched television. While they lived at the hotel Cindy attended Head Start. Going to school seemed to be a welcome relief from life at the hotel. She said, "It was a nice school." She recalled her routine there very well,

> A little bus came and picks me up. We eat breakfast first, then we have a little play time, then we have lunch, then we take a nap. When our teachers come back from lunch then we got up and we ate snack. She gave us another play time and then the bus came and got us.

Cindy said that she likes living in the current shelter. "I think it's nice. The people is nice to me. The one's on my floor. Wendy next door to my mother and Ann by the steps. They help Mommy with me and Dana."

Cindy attends Kindergarten near the shelter. She said that she likes "to play dolls" with her friends and to "learn my ABC's and 123's." She seems proud that she has learned to write and spell her name and demonstrated her skill for me.

Cindy enjoys going to her aunt's house where she is able to play outside more than at the shelter. She said,

> I got two ropes. I have a long one and a short one. I don't play with them when my mommy don't go outside. When she do go outside I take them with me. When we go to my aunt's house I take them outside and play with my cousins. At my aunt's house she has a front yard and a back yard. So if we don't go in the back we could go in the front and that way our aunt could see us what we do.

INTRODUCTION TO THE GONZALEZ FAMILY

The Gonzalez family consists of Isabel and her two children Jose age 13, and Christina age 11. Isabel also has a 19 year old son who lives in Puerto Rico. Isabel and her children have been in the shelter system for approximately fifteen months and have lived in the current shelter for eight months. The Gonzalez family share a one bedroom apartment which was very clean on the first visit and more messy on the second. They have two sofas in the living room and a television set with Nintendo. Isabel and Christina sleep in the bedroom while Jose sleeps in the living room.

All family members were interviewed for the study. Interviews took place in the living room of their apartment. Everyone was interviewed twice with second interviews conducted primarily for clarification. Isabel and Christina's first interviews lasted an hour while Jose's interview was thirty minutes. Second interviews were shorter, thirty minutes for Isabel and Christina and fifteen minutes for Jose.

Profile of Isabel Gonzalez

Isabel as a participant in the study. Isabel is a 40 year old overweight Hispanic woman. She is asthmatic and suffers with migraine headaches. Isabel grew up in Puerto Rico. She is separated from her husband who still lives there. She eagerly agreed to participate in the study and stated that she had many stories to tell. When I looked for her to set up the first appointment, her daughter told me I could find her at work in the mailroom. I had no trouble locating her there, and she proudly showed me her place of work and introduced me to co-workers and to her boss. Isabel made arrangements to change her work schedule so she could be interviewed.

Spanish is Isabel's first language. Although she speaks English fairly well, a heavy accent makes it difficult to understand her at times. She spoke freely about her experience and grew upset and agitated while telling her story. She smoked throughout the interview.

Isabel's experience. Isabel has moved back and forth between New York and Puerto Rico several times. Her parents and the rest of her family live there. Isabel and her children were living in Puerto Rico for two years before she decided to return to New York where she had previously lived for five years. In Puerto Rico they lived with her father in a large house. Isabel described the reasons for these moves:

> I was sick, I got so much asthma. Then my mother was sick, too, so I went over there to see if I can't find a job there. But I couldn't find nothing. There's no work there. So I was having a hard time. Money. So I came back to New York.

Isabel returned to New York with money that she thought would be sufficient to find an apartment. She said,

> The last time it wasn't hard. But now the rent increases. The rents. I can't pay $600 for three rooms. Welfare doesn't pay that amount. So it was hard. I can't find an apartment. I got money because I make a lot in Puerto Rico and I bring a lot of money, $1300.

Isabel initially stayed with a man with whom she was involved before she left New York. She said he was part of the reason she returned to New York but "it didn't work the same way I thought it was going to work. So I decide to go away then and I go away and that's it." She said she does not see him anymore. Isabel was reluctant to talk about this man and initially said they stayed with "a relative" when they first came back to New York. However, the children's account of living with their mother's "boyfriend" led me to question her further.

Isabel said that when she entered the shelter system she initially had trouble finding a placement because her son is older and placed in a class for emotionally disturbed children. She said,

> I went to my center. And my caseworker, then she found me a place in Brooklyn. They didn't want to accept me because the kid was way too big. They sent me to EAU. And then they send me overnight to another shelter. The next day they send me again to the shelter and they say they can't leave me sleeping in that shelter because my son is disabled and disturbed. So they tell me that they have to find me a hotel. And they found a hotel for me [then] they closed the hotel. I was seven

> months living there.   They closed it and they
> transferred me here.

Isabel said that living in the hotel for seven months was "a big disaster." She described the problems:

> Stuck in the room, the people, different kinds of
> people, seeing all those druggies. Everything was
> bad over there. Everything, Everything. . . The room
> it was so little for my daughter, me and my son, it
> was too crowded.

Isabel feels that she and her children suffered several major consequences due to their homelessness and exposure to the hotel environment. She said:

> They sell every kind of drug. I almost destroyed
> myself too because I started drinking, drinking,
> drinking. I can't take it. I can't live here in the
> hotel, I can't, I can't. I don't know what I'm going
> to do one of these days. Sometimes I think stupid
> things, I think I'm going to kill myself. Because I
> can't take it, I can't be living in all that insanity.
> For me it was a big disaster. And then all the
> things that affect me affected the children.
> Because they saw me, saw me crying, sometimes
> anger. So that affected them too.

Yet, Isabel was able to overcome her despair. She said that she stopped drinking. She recalled, "But then one day I look in the mirror. I said, what the hell you doing with you life. . . So by myself I stopped. " She became involved with a support group run by an outside agency for single parents.

While she was living in the hotel, Isabel placed her son in a group foster home because, "his behavior was changing." She explained,

> He ain't got place to play in the room because it
> was too little. So he was hanging out in the hall
> and everything. The people was giving complaints.
> So I just had to place him until I could have my
> own place.

She was able to take him out of foster care when she moved into this shelter. However, she said that she continues to have difficulty with him. She is taking him for counseling at an outside agency, but said "nothing helps." At the time of the interview he was refusing to go to school at all. She said that she does not like his friends, one of whom is on trial for selling drugs, and may place him in foster care again.

In contrast, Isabel seemed very proud of her daughter who she said gives her no trouble and is doing very well in school. "I'd sit down with her and I could talk to her. Because she understands me more than he does. She has more capacity because she understands."

Isabel said she is happier with the current shelter:

> This place is the best. They help you a lot in here. They have self-help, coping group, life management, how to manage your budget. They help you a lot. They got everything, counseling for kids. They have after-school programs.

Isabel was particularly proud of her participation in the job training program at the shelter. She usually works three hours a day in the mailroom and is paid for her work. However, most of the money she earns goes into a special account so that her welfare benefits are not affected. She will be able to use the money to buy furniture and other things once she moves out of the shelter. She said about her job:

> It's nice. I like it. And when I move out of here they going to find me good work, a good job, like maybe in word processing because I have some skill in the computer." She added, "I learned a lot, especially about mail. And we take tutoring on Thursday and Tuesday and I take computer class on Thursday and Friday too.

Isabel expressed the wish to leave the current shelter because of conflicts with some of the other residents. She said that all her friends had moved away already, and she only has a few friends left in the mailroom where she works. She was upset because:

> Somebody called BCW (Bureau of Child Welfare)
> for me. They say that I'm an alcoholic and I
> cocaine it big. That I don't feed my kids, that I
> used to beat them up. That I abuse them. . . the
> one that call is the one that is a crack addict.

She added that these women:

> All the time they're begging for cigarettes, begging
> for food, begging for everything. The whole day.
> So I say stop begging me. I ain't got nothing,
> nobody gave me nothing. So I had to stop it. So
> now they mad because of that.

Isabel said that the workers sent to investigate found no truth to
the claim. However, she said, "I was crying. I had a breakdown. I
can't sleep. I can't eat thinking they going to remove my kids for no
reason."   However, she felt the workers at the shelter were
supportive and helped her through the situation by defending her and
meeting with her afterwards.

Since this incident Isabel is particularly anxious to move out.
She would like to live in the public housing projects but feels it will
take too long to be accepted because she has to follow special
procedures since her son is classified as emotionally disturbed.
Instead, Isabel is pursuing apartments through a nonprofit
organization that renovates apartments for the homeless. At the
time of the last interview, she had just heard about a three bedroom
apartment in the Bronx which she hoped would be acceptable.

Profile of Christina Gonzalez

Christina as a participant in the study.   Christina is a pretty 11
year old girl who is overweight. She said that she is enuretic. She
eagerly agreed to participate in the study.   Christina seemed to be
lonely and to enjoy the opportunity to talk about her experience.

While I interviewed her mother and brother I was able to
observe Christina's behavior at home. She frequently fought with
her brother when he was home. She played Nintendo while I was
there the first time and watched television the second time.

Christina's experience.   Christina said they left Puerto Rico
"because my mother didn't like it over there. And she was too sick.

And they didn't have that much medication and everything." She recalled staying with her "stepfather" when they first returned to New York. She said, "We went to my stepfather's house. So we stayed there. Not really my stepfather you know." She continued:

> So we stayed there and then my mother and him had an argument. I don't know why it was. And my brother cursed him out. So he got mad. So we went to his brother's house. His brother is drunk. He's a drunk person, alcoholic person, so he threw us out of there.

Christina described being sent from place to place by the EAU when they first entered the shelter system. She said that they were sent to places but the EAU didn't call ahead to let the shelter or hotel know they were coming so they were turned away when they got there. She said:

> First I went to this Brooklyn hotel. And they said that they don't want us there. So we went back to the EAU. And the cab, the taxi driver took our stuff because we didn't have no money to pay him. So he took our TV, our little TV, and our clothes.

Christina said that after leaving the Brooklyn hotel they were sent to several shelters for one night until her mother told EAU that her brother had been placed in a foster home. Then EAU found them a place in a hotel, but when they got there the hotel was not expecting them. She explained what happened:

> And welfare, they send us to the hotel and they told us that they wasn't supposed to get us but they gave my mother a favor. Because the welfare didn't tell them nothing. So they did my mother the favor so we stayed there for seven months.

About the hotel she said:

> It was kind of okay. I didn't like it because it was too little and we couldn't bring no stove in there, no refrigerators or nothing. My mother sneaked in this little refrigerator, and when there was inspection, she put a table cloth and made believe

that was a little table. And she bought this little
thing like a stove. And my mother bought pots and
cups and everything. And then every they used to
come, my mother used to hide it.

She added, "I didn't like it that much. I didn't feel like it was
really my house."

Christina felt that the larger hotel next door was dangerous but
that their hotel was relatively safe. She said, "they used to kill
there and everything." She described what she did after school
while living in the hotel:

I go out and play with my friends. We went out to
the afterschools. We went to this place, we used
to swim there and everything. And sometimes we
used to come from school, we used to stay in the
halls playing sometimes. They used to come to
my house, I used to go to their house.

Christina said that she likes where they are staying now. She
said, "I feel like this is my house. And I don't want to move out of
here. I really don't. But we're going to have to."

Christina has been placed in three schools since returning to
New York. She said that she has always done well in school and
was in a program for gifted students in Puerto Rico. She attended
first and second grade in New York and third and fourth grade in
Puerto Rico. She came to New York in the middle of fourth grade
but said she was not promoted to fifth grade that year because her
ability to read English was below grade level.

Christina said that she no longer has any friends who live at the
shelter but she has friends in school.

My number one best friend is my mother. And the
other two are Francis in my school, in my class,
she's my best friend. And my other friend moved
out of here, Linda. And I got more friends in
school, almost the whole school knows me.

Christina said that some of her friends in school say negative things
about where she lives. She said,

Some of my friends say I'm never going to live in a
shelter. I don't like to live in a shelter. Like that.

> And they said that they don't like shelters or
> nothing. They never come and live in it. And I
> feel bad.

Christina said that sometimes she does not feel like going to
school and stays home.

> And sometimes when I don't want to go to school
> and I feel sick, and my mother lets me stay here, I
> just do it. And when I don't want to go to school,
> I'll tell my mother that I will fix up her house, the
> whole house. And when she comes home, the
> house is all messed up.

For example, she said that she did not want to go to school on
the days they have gym class because they are being punished. She
feels that this punishment is her fault. She said, "And that's not fair
because I fell down the stairs and they're going to come and blame
it on everybody." Another time she did not want to go to school
because she was afraid some kids were going to "jump" her because
of a rumor to that effect. She said that sometimes she does not want
to go to school because she has no clean clothes to wear.

After school she said that she usually attends an after school
program then comes home and eats, sleeps, watches television and
plays Nintendo. She has one good friend, Linda, who moved out of
the shelter. Christina enjoys visiting her in her new apartment on
weekends.

> We have a lot of fun because she takes us out.
> She takes us to the restaurants. She let us see TV.
> And we play over there. We have fun a lot.
> Because she got her own room and everything.
> And her mother got her own room and her two
> brothers share a room. And we have fun. And we
> be seeing movies, on the VCR we see movies.

Christina expressed a number of worries:

> I don't know what I would do if my mother dies.
> And I worry if I become fat. And if we don't get
> our apartment. I worry if we don't get no money. I
> worry how we be able to dress nice. I worry, God
> forbid, they kill or anything here. I worry if we get

our apartment I won't be able to see my best friend again.

Christina's hopes for the future include wishes for herself, her family and the world in general. She said:

> My mother and I dress nice and be skinny, slender.
> I dress nice with nice clothes, nice coats. And I
> want to see my best friend. And I would like to
> see my brother behave better. And I really hope
> my mother will stay here now. And I would like to
> see people helping each other. I wouldn't let
> anybody be homeless. There would be no homes
> in the street. There won't be no killing. And there
> would be no drugs.

Profile of Jose Gonzalez

Jose as a participant in the study. Jose is an overweight thirteen year old boy who looks older than his stated age. He agreed to participate in the study, although somewhat reluctantly. He answered most questions, but his answers were generally brief. He seemed to feel more comfortable during the second interview when some of his answers were more candid and elaborate. During the interview, he looked out the window for his friend and when he saw him called to him. He seemed impatient for the interview to be over and ran out to play football as soon as it was finished.

Jose's experience. Jose said that they left Puerto Rico because "my mother wanted to be with her husband." He said this with a very contemptuous tone in his voice. He later referred to his mother's husband as his cousin. They all moved in with this man who lived in a studio apartment. He explained why this arrangement did not work: "Where we used to live in the Bronx we had problems with the landlord. That's when we became homeless. He used to say I write on the walls but I never did. We had to leave."

Jose said that he liked the hotel they moved to after leaving the apartment in the Bronx. He described what he used to do while they lived in the hotel:

> Writing in the halls, writing on the wall, breaking
> into rooms. We used to ride the freight elevator. It

> was boring so we had nothing to do. There was
> nothing else to do.

He described riding on the top of the elevator with his friends.

> We used to play around in the elevator. Get in top.
> You know how you open the elevator on the top
> with a little door. We used to go up there. We
> had fun doing that. We could play with it, make
> the elevator go up and down because there were
> some buttons on top.

Jose said that he used to break into rooms at night so he could sleep by himself in his own bed. He said that otherwise he had to share a bed with his sister or sleep on a mattress on the floor. He said, "it was real uncomfortable. It was a hard mattress. It was better living in the street. You got more room."

When asked how he felt about how upset his mother was while living in the hotel, he said, "I didn't really care because I was having fun." While he said he was having fun, he also said, "I wanted to leave." When his mother decided to place him in foster care he did not seem to mind. He said, "It was a lot better. I had my own bed. My own room."

Jose's mother took him out of foster care when she moved to the current shelter. He is currently in a class for emotionally disturbed children. He said he was placed in that class because, "I disrespect teachers. I clown a lot. " During the first interview he said, "I don't like school. Too much writing. It's boring. I get tired from doing all the work." He complained about English class and writing. He said that "math is my best subject." On the day of the second interview, Jose told me that he did not want to go back to school. He had just finished a one-week suspension. He said, "I got suspended because I had a fight. We had an argument and he stabbed me with a pencil." When asked what the argument was about, Jose said that he did not remember. Instead of returning to that school, Jose said that he would like to go back into foster care where he thought the school was better.

Jose's difficulties in school are of long duration. When the family lived in New York previously, his mother tried sending him back to Puerto Rico twice to live with relatives when she had difficulty with him. She also had placed him in a foster home when he returned to her after continuing to have difficulty in Puerto Rico. He said, he returned to Puerto Rico when he was nine years old after two years in New York because, "I was having problems in school so my mother sent me to Puerto Rico to see if I would do better." He said:

> I went back when I was nine years old and stayed there for eight months. Then I came back with my mother. Then I went back for four months. I couldn't handle it so I came back. I tried to stay over there for school. I couldn't make it. I forgot my Spanish. I couldn't go through that Spanish class.

It seems that switching between school in Puerto Rico and New York has left Jose lacking skills in both English and Spanish. Although Jose felt the school in the foster home was better, he said that he likes living in the current shelter more than the foster home. He said, "I have more freedom here than over there." He said that he does not want to move out because, "I like it. My mother wants to but not me. I like this place."

Jose has attended four different schools, including the one in the foster home, since they returned to New York. He said, "The hardest thing for me is making friends. That's all. It's hard for me, making new friends moving from one place to another and having to make new friends."

Jose's best friend, Hector, lives in the projects across the street from the shelter and is much older than he. Hector is nineteen and graduating from high school this year. Jose said, "I hate hanging around with little kids my age. I just don't like it." He met his friend, Hector and other older boys outside playing football. He said about Hector, "I be with my friend everyday. We go visit his family house and hang out. Almost everyday we go. We like traveling that's what we do."

Jose participates in some activities at the shelter. He went to summer camp there. About the camp he said, "They treat us like little kids. They treat us like five, six years old. I didn't like it. I went for two or three months. It was boring." When asked what they did there, he said, "They took us to Bear Mountain, they took us to seven lakes, they took us to the zoo, took us to movies, to the museum. While he admitted some of the trips were interesting, he said, I'd rather be outside with my friends." However, he also sometimes joins the group for recreational activities on Saturdays. He said, "Every Saturday they take us around to skating, museums places like that. Sometimes when they go skating I go with them."

Jose said that he has to "behave" to help his family move out of the shelter. He acknowledges that his problems in school "affect the apartment because the place we move to wants to know if I go to school and stuff like that. They want a report from my school how I do in school." However, he seems to be unable or unwilling to improve his situation there. He added, "I don't like that school. I just don't like it."

Jose said that his mother tries to help him: "My mom. That's the only person that tried to help me a lot. She gives advice and talks to me a lot. Sometimes I listen to her and sometimes I don't."

In the future, Jose would like to be a football player or a veterinarian. He said he would like to be a veterinarian because, "I love animals. In Puerto Rico I had pet dogs, chickens, ducks and roosters. I had two birds here too but they flew out of this window." He would like to be a football player because, "I like to play. I got a trophy. I was on the teams in the foster home. Baseball, soccer, football, I was on the swimming team too." In addition to his personal plans, Jose would like to see "drugs stopped. That's all I really want to see. Peace in the world."

INTRODUCTION TO THE JONES FAMILY

The Jones family consists of Sylvia and her four children, Alison, age 8, Jackie, age 6, Jason, age 5 and Lisa, age 3. Sylvia is pregnant with her fifth child. They have been in the shelter system for four and one half months and have already been contacted for an apartment.

The family shares a one bedroom apartment. The children sleep in the living room and their mother has the bedroom. Interviews took place in the living room of their apartment which was clean. The children's clothes looked very worn and had some holes in them. The children had few toys to play with and mostly seemed to watch television.

Sylvia and the three oldest children were interviewed for the study. Sylvia was interviewed twice while the children were each interviewed once. I visited the family on two occasions and interviewed one to two children and their mother on each visit. One interview seemed sufficient for the children and two seemed necessary for the mother as certain issues needed clarification after the first interview.

Profile of Sylvia Jones

Sylvia's as a participant in the study. Sylvia is a twenty-four year
old Black woman. When Sylvia was a young child, her mother died
leaving her to be raised by her grandmother. Sylvia completed
eighth grade but never went to high school. She was pregnant with
her first child at age 16. She tried several times to return to school
to get training in office work as well as her GED. However, each
time her studies seemed to be interrupted when she had another
child. Her first three children have the same father. Her fourth
child has a different father to whom Sylvia was married briefly. Her
unborn child has another father, a man from Brooklyn whom she
continues to see.

Sylvia eagerly agreed to participate in the study. She is two
months pregnant with her fifth child. Sylvia lay on the couch and
sucked her thumb during most of the interview. Still, she spoke
freely about her experience.

Sylvia's experience. Sylvia lived with her grandmother and
three brothers, ages 20, 23, and 26, in a large apartment in a public
housing project in Brooklyn. In that apartment, she had her own
room and the children shared a room. She described the living
situation there:

> I was living with my grandmother. I was paying
> rent there. My grandmother wouldn't allow me to
> have company in her house. I was buying food
> there. And my brothers done did what they wanted
> to do there. It was all right for them to do what
> they wanted to do. They can bring company,
> whoever they want to there. And she allowed them
> to. But I couldn't do nothing. Because I'm the girl.
> The boys can do everything. And I'm still a kid to
> her. I ain't never growed up. That's the way she
> take me. I'm still fifteen. I'm the oldest girl and
> she still takes me as a baby.

Sylvia described her decision to leave:

> And well, we wasn't getting along so I got tired of
> living with her. Me and my brothers weren't
> getting along. I was buying food and they were
> eating it like dogs. And half of the time, they

> would just eat it and they didn't have no courtesy
> for the children. it's there and let's eat it. That's
> how they was. And wanted my privacy. So I left
> home.

Sylvia had applied for her own apartment while living with her
grandmother. She had no success. She said:

> I had an application in housing but they didn't give
> me my own apartment. They just kept me and my
> grandmother together. They moved her from one
> project to another projects, bigger projects, and let
> all of us stay together. And we were not getting
> along to be together. I'm grown. She's grown. We
> all need our own.

After she left her grandmother's house she said they went to the
Emergency Assistance Unit. She continued:

> And we stayed there all night. Then somewhere in
> Manhattan they sent us at six o'clock in the
> morning. For us to go there and spend the rest of
> the day and then come back to EAU. So what I
> did, instead of go over to Manhattan, I went back
> home to my grandmother's house. Stayed there
> and then go back to EAU again at five o'clock that
> evening. So the kids won't miss the day out of
> school. So then about four o'clock in the morning
> again they moved us to the Bronx. And we was in
> the Bronx for two weeks.

Sylvia described what it was like at the barracks shelter in the
Bronx.

> No privacy. It was weird. Because I wasn't used
> to living around people. I had to sleep in clothes.
> You couldn't get comfortable like you would do at
> your own house.

She said that the children had no trouble sleeping in the shelter but
that she sometimes did. She said,

Oh, they went to sleep. Because at nine o'clock
they cut all the lights off. We had to go to sleep,
so they went to bed. They had little cots. They all
had one bed for each one of the children. They
took they showers and went to bed. They didn't
complain about that. Sometime I didn't sleep. I
stayed up because it's uncomfortable when you
have to watch the children. Because they had
women there with they men and all of that. So you
had to keep your eyes open. So I kept my pants on,
stuff like that. And kept my eyes open. Because
you don't know what will happen in a place like
that. Anything could happen. Even though they
had guards there.

She reported that the rules made her uncomfortable and the
food made the children sick:

And we had to take time, sign to wash, sign to
borrow an iron. And they food kept getting the kids
sick. It was like TV food. And every time they
start eating it, after the first week, they got sick.
They kept vomiting and vomiting. And they kept
giving them medicine for it and they wouldn't stop.
So then I started taking them to restaurants. And
they was alright then. They didn't get sick no
more. So I figure it was the shelter's food.

Sylvia made sure her children did not miss any school while
they were in the shelter. However, since they were placed so far
from their old neighborhood in Brooklyn getting them there required
a long subway trip. She said:

Then I had to get up every morning, six o'clock in
the morning to take them to Brooklyn to school.
They got there on time. It took an hour and a half
but I got them up early so they can get dressed, get
there. Take them to school, take my three year old
with me to my girl friend's house, go sit in my girl
friend's house to three o'clock, go pick them back
up and then go back to the Bronx. That's how we
was doing every day. Until they moved us over
here, then I transferred them from Brooklyn to here.

Sylvia did not seem to feel that her children really minded staying at the shelter. She said,

> They didn't complain about nothing. There were glad from being where they was at. All the kids knew them. I didn't mingle with nobody. I just stayed to myself. Just like I do here. I stay mostly to myself. I was just going in and out. I was just mostly there on weekends. That's the only time we mostly there. It was boring because there was nothing for them to do. And you couldn't make them run around all day. They had to stay down, stuff like that.

Sylvia said that she was able to get the family transferred to the current shelter because she knew something about the different kinds of shelters. She said:

> I talked to a worker from the Bronx and I had asked him a lot about Tier II. I heard about Tier II in Brooklyn. My girlfriend was telling me about it. So he told me he didn't have a Tier II for my family size in Brooklyn but he had one in Manhattan. Do I want it? And I said, Oh sure. And that's how I got here. I didn't want to go to a hotel. He wanted to put me in a hotel by the airport and I told him how would the kids get to school. I told him no, I couldn't go there.

Sylvia seemed to like it better in the current shelter than in the previous one. In comparison she said, "We can go in and out. And they are like home here. This is like home. That's the only difference. They have like they own private house." In addition she added,

> Everybody here is friendly. The workers are pretty nice. You can speak to them about anything and they will talk to you, give their opinions on it. So they're like a big family here. That's all. That's why it's nice. She said, "living here doesn't make you feel like you're homeless.

The only negative consequence Sylvia associated with the family becoming homeless was how her son's behavior in school. The school wants Jason evaluated for a special education class for emotionally disturbed children but she does not want the evaluation to take place. She feels the school is to blame since he has been in daycare and school before and never had problems.

> He fights over there a lot and they keep calling me over there. And now they tell me for him to see a psychiatrist and all that. And I'm telling them they wasting my time with that. I'm not taking him to no psychiatrist. He don't act like this at no other school so why all of a sudden at this school he's terrorizing the whole school. They make him sound like he's a screech owl, that's running around loose out there and all type of garbage. Like he's just coming to school and tearing everybody up, beating everybody up and all that junk. That's the only thing make me angry. I don't like that school at all.

Sylvia still sees the father of her unborn child. He visits her at the shelter several times a week. She said that he gives her some financial help. She said:

> At times he gives me some money. I really don't ask him because he has his own family to deal with. But he gives me. And he has rent to pay where he lives at and all of that stuff. But when he gives I take it. He has four children. But his children are older than mines. But they live with their grandmother. He visits them and stuff.

Sylvia has a good friend from her old neighborhood in Brooklyn with whom she occasionally stays on weekends. Her friend has been helpful to her since she entered the shelter system. She used to spend the day there when her children were at school while waiting to pick them up. Her friend also told her about the different types of shelters so she was able to ask for the current placement. Sylvia said she sometimes visits her brothers and sisters on the weekends but stays with her friend.

At the shelter, Sylvia sometimes attends the meetings and plans to start a job providing child care for parents who attend meetings at the shelter. She would get paid for this job. She baby-sits for another woman who pays her "whatever she can give me." She said that her social worker is helping her find an apartment. For example, "housing needs certain papers. She'll get in touch with me and tell me to get certain papers."

For the future, she would like to go back to school. She says, "I will find a school near my way, whatever. Once the baby gets six months, I know I'm going to put him in day care and maybe go back to school."

Profile of Alison Jones

Alison as a participant in the study. Alison is a pretty, eight year old Black girl with braided hair. Her clothes were worn and tattered. She agreed to participate in the study and answered most questions presented. She seemed unhappy and depressed. She grew sad as she talked about her experience and started to cry. When I visited the family the second time she was sleeping as her mother says she often does when she gets home from school.

Alison's experience. Alison said that she did not want to leave the apartment her mother shared with her great-grandmother. She said the hardest thing has been "because my mother said we couldn't go back there. And I want to go back." She said, "I wanted to stay with my grandmother because she gave me more than my mother gave me. She added, "Because she's old and everything. I wanted to stay with her." She recalled crying when her mother told her she was leaving and started to cry while she talked about it. Her mother said that Alison is very close to her great-grandmother, and with her sister had spent a year living with her in Jamaica.

After leaving their apartment Alison recalled:

> I went to some kind of shelter. And when we went there, they told us we had to go somewhere else. And then my mother didn't went there. She went back to my grandmother's house. And then we went back there. Then, that time we went where that person said we were supposed to go. And then after that I don't know where we went but we went to some other shelter. And then we went to the subway to go to the Bronx. And then, after we went to the Bronx we came here.

Alison did not seem to mind the shelter in the Bronx too much. She said, "It was not too bad because I knew a lot of friends there. And I met new friends. About five." She did not seem to mind the long trip to her school in Brooklyn from the Bronx. She said she liked the school in Brooklyn better than the one she goes to now. She feels she learned more there:

> And the kids over here, they punch and curse at the teacher and curse. And the teachers don't do nothing. But over at my other school they went to go to the principal. And these principals don't do nothing. And my other principal, they used to do stuff. I didn't want to go to this school. I wanted to stay at my other school. But my mother said, No.

Alison said she was sometimes tired in school while she lived at the shelter in the Bronx. She said,

> Because I used to always stay up. I be dreaming but not very good dreams. And then I stays up because it looked like I'm broken, it looked like I was all over the place. I was dreaming about monsters and everything.

In contrast, Alison said that she no longer has bad dreams in the current shelter. However, she seemed to have mixed feelings about the children who live there. She said, "I like a lot of people that live here in this building and other buildings. I know a lot of people." She has some friends from the shelter with whom she goes to school . However, she said, "I don't go outside anymore. Because I don't want to go outside because they don't like me because I'm black and they want to beat me up so I don't want to go outside."

Alison also said that some children that do not live in the shelter tease her.

> They say that's why you live in the Castle and that's why you poor. They call this the castle. But some of my friends don't say I'm poor because they say I don't look like I'm poor. I don't like when people call me poor. But I'm not poor.

However, Alison does seem to feel deprived. She said,

> I don't have a lot of things that I want. And my
> mother say that you can't get a lot because you're
> not rich. But I understand and I don't ask her for
> nothing. Only sometimes when she have her
> money.

On weekends, Alison said that she watches television, does chores, reads and daydreams. She said, "I watch TV and sometimes I don't read that much because we have to do things that we have to do in the house. And I don't have a lot of time. Only sometimes my mother tell me that we not watching TV and day dreaming." When asked what she day dreams about she said, "Like I have people in my family that passed away and everything. And I never saw my grandmother. Because my grandmother died when my mother was six years old so I ain't getting a chance to meet no more grandmother, only knew her on a picture."

Alison is currently in third grade at the public school located near the shelter. She has never been left back. She said that she likes school because:

> It's interesting and it makes me learn more things
> than I know. I learn to read and my math and read
> a lot so I take a lot of tests and try my best to do
> lots of things. And try to get 100's and stuff on our
> tests.

She does not like school because, "it's boys. It's boys are bad and everything. And yelling and everything and I can't learn a lot of things that I'm supposed to learn."

Alison attends an after school program at her school Monday through Thursday afternoons. She said that she eats dinner there and often completes her homework too. She says, "I like it because it's like different teachers that you meet that I don't know when I go to regular school. And I meet new friends."

Alison said that her mother and her friends help her when things are hard for her. She said her mother helps "because when I tell her some things some time, she do it for me sometimes. And when I tell her sometimes, she don't do it." She says her friends help too. "They tell me more things that I never know. About friends. And sometimes they tell me what to do and not to do."

When she grows up Alison would like to be "a doctor, a singer and a dancer." She plans to do this "by growing up, get an education and working and things." She would like to live "in Brooklyn or Jamaica." She would like to live in "Jamaica in the islands. Because I like it better because my cousins live over there. Or I like to live where the Spanish people live. Because some of my cousins live over there. And I want to know how to learn Spanish."

Profile of Jackie Jones

Jackie as a participant in the study. Jackie is a pretty six year old girl with neatly braided hair. At the time of the interview, she was missing her two front teeth. Like her sister, Jackie's clothes were somewhat worn and patched. She was interviewed in the living room of her family's apartment at the shelter. Jackie eagerly agreed to participate in the study. She was proud of her school work and shared it with me. However, it was difficult for her to remain focused and seated for the duration of the interview. Jackie's recall of information and events was somewhat vague, but her awareness of her feelings was very clear.

Jackie's experience. Jackie said they left her great-grandmother's apartment:

> Cause her and my aunt was talking about my ma saying that she don't help her kids, she always leave her kids in the house. She don't even care about her kids. All kind of that stuff. . . I wanted to stay with my grandmother.

Jackie remembered going to the barracks shelter after leaving her great-grandmother's house. She thought it was "fine" and liked that "they let you run around sometimes" She remembered going to school in Brooklyn by train but her memories did not seem particularly clear. She said it did not take long to get there and only recalled taking one train. Her mother said the trip took an hour and a half and that they took two or three trains. Jackie said she "went to grandma's house" after school where she waited "until Mommy come pick us up." She said she did not mind going back to the shelter afterwards because, "it was nice there." The only problem was the food because "the food made me sick."

Jackie seemed happy with the current shelter. She said, "I like this place but I don't like that school." She added, "it's nice. We go outside and play right out there. Sometimes we see movies downstairs."

Jackie said the hardest thing for her has been "going to a new school." She said, "it make me feel angry. I don't like moving around to different schools." Jackie has mixed feelings about her current school. She says that she does not like it because,

> They don't do nothing when kids bother other kids.
> They think we bothering them. And they don't do
> nothing to them but they do something to
> somebody else. Cause they think that we bothering
> them but they bothering us. Then the teacher be
> saying that's me fighting all the kids. She says
> that she fights with the other kids because of things
> they say, They say F word. They put up they
> middle finger at me. They say we live in a castle.
> And they say we poor. And they say we can't
> dress.

Jackie said that she feels angry when they say that and fights them. She said, "I had three fights today. Because these kids were bothering me."

However, Jackie also says, "I like my teacher. Cause she nice. She let us play." She showed me a folder of her work from school and seemed particularly proud of a book the other children had made for her when she was "star of the week." The book was filled with drawings from the other children in her classroom with messages explaining why they like Jackie. For example, one drawing said, "I like Jackie because she plays with her friends", another said "I like Jackie because she dresses nice." Jackie said that she has a lot of friends in school. She said, "My friends help me do my work. They help me when I get in fights."

Jackie seemed to be looking forward to moving to a new apartment but is very conflicted about her wish to live with her mother and grandmother. For example, she drew a picture of herself moving into a new house. She said she was happy "cause I'm moving" and "because I live in the house and I didn't want to live with my grandmother. My grandmother is mean to me." She is also worried about the new children she will meet. She said, "When we lived in Brooklyn last time we had a fight with some kids." She seemed worried the same thing might happen again. When she grows up Jackie would like to be "a singer, a dancer and a nurse."

Jackie said that she liked it in Jamaica and would like to live there. Jackie would also like to live in Queens. She said, I like to live in Queens cause my cousin, my uncle live in Queens. She said, "they live in a big house." She said she would like to live in Queens or Jamaica.

Profile of Jason Jones

Jason as a participant in the study. Jason is a cute five year old boy who seemed very excited about being interviewed. He fought with his sisters over who would be interviewed first. He wanted to hear himself on the tape recorder almost as soon as the interview began but was able to wait until the interview was finished. He is very active and had a difficult time sitting still while being interviewed. He was easily distracted and got up often. He needed frequent redirection and refocusing. He sat very close to me during the interview and seemed to want to maintain physical contact. He answered the interview questions to the best of his ability. He grew sad and looked like he might cry when he talked about his great-grandmother.

Jason's experience. Jason said they left his great-grandmother's house "cause they were talking about my mother." He grew tearful. "I can't say the kind of words." He said,

> I don't like my grandmother cause she be saying
> curses to us and she be terrible to my mother. I
> don't like my uncles cause they be saying it too. I
> can't say the curses they say.

However, Jason is conflicted about his grandmother and uncles for whom he maintains strong positive feelings. Jason said that the hardest thing for him has been missing his great-grandmother. He said,

> I feel bad cause I want to go back there. I miss
> them. My mother didn't want me to go see her. I
> couldn't. I miss grandma. Her in Jamaica with my
> cousin. She's been there a lot of years.

Although it may feel like years to Jason, according to his mother she has only been there a few months and will back in the summer.

Jason also said he misses his cousin who lived with them until three months ago. He said:

> They stole my cousin. His father came and took him. He lied. I cried. His mother told his father to take him. He said he was going to bring him back here. He didn't bring him back.

After leaving his great-grandmother's house, Jason recalled they went to "the Bronx. I came to the shelter." He thought it was "good. They gave you food and stuff. We play and go to bed." He said he liked the food but "we be throwing up" He added that he "ran around and stuff and played with my friends" and "I didn't want to move."

Jason recalled the trip to school in Brooklyn while they were at the shelter in the Bronx:

> My mommy took me. I took a train and a bus to get there. Then she leave us. It was a long time. I saw the water. We was on a bridge. We got up early in the morning, and I had to get dressed. My sisters they didn't want to go cause it was raining. We went one time when it was raining cause we wanted to go. It was a long walk to get to the train station. A very, very long walk.

Jason is in kindergarten at the public school near the shelter. According to his mother he has been fighting in school. Jason seemed to have strong feelings about his current school. He said, "I don't like this school. It's real backwards." He seemed to sense that they want to place him in special education. He said that he does not like it, "Cause it's boring. Cause they being bad. Cause they don't want me in school. They told me, I ain't in that school. The teacher said he ain't in this class."

When asked why he fights he said, referring to some children who go to his school, "I be mad when they be beating up my sisters. I hit them back. My friends help me fight too." He added, "they say curses, they say the letter a, they talking bad about my mother, the say f your house." He said he feels "real bad when they be messing with my sisters. They put up their middle fingers at my sister."

However, he also has some positive feelings for his teacher and his class. He says "I like my teacher." She "help us with our work.

Give us homework." He says that he likes some of the kids in school and they help "when I be doing my work." He likes to do "any kind" of work and likes to play "blocks, I build a store and a castle."

Jason seemed to like the current shelter. He said that he would like to live there. He said, "I like to play with my friends. I be happy when I play with my friends." He said that he has a friend who lives downstairs. He likes to play hide and seek with him. Like his sisters, Jason attends an afterschool program four afternoons per week. He said, "I play the kitchen and the blocks, puzzles and color." When he gets home he likes to "sleep and eat and watch TV." On the weekends he likes to "play with my cars." Sometimes he says he visits his uncles and aunts in Brooklyn. Jason looked forward to moving to their new apartment in Brooklyn. He said, "got my own room, getting a VCR, watch tapes, watch recorded tapes." He said he thought he would like it there "If I don't go to that same school."

V

Results: Thematic Analysis

This chapter presents the categories and themes that emerged from the analysis of interviews with mothers and children who participated in this study. Categories serve to organize themes around certain central issues. Themes are affect-laden statements which appear frequently across interviews or seem particularly relevant and important.

CATEGORY I: BECOMING HOMELESS - THE STORY

Theme A: *I Had No Choice, I Was Forced to Leave.*

Two of the six mothers reported that they were evicted from their apartments by their landlord. Maria felt that her landlord and welfare worked together to evict her. She said that the landlord told her the apartment was too big for her family size and welfare told her the rent was too high. Evelyn said that her landlord evicted her because she said she wanted the apartment for her own family.

Theme B: *I Decided to Leave So We Could Have a Better Life.*

Four of the six mothers left their apartments in an effort to improve their situation. Three of these mothers assumed they would be able to find affordable housing and were surprised when they were unable to do so. Linda and Isabel came to New York from Puerto Rico. Linda said she left an abusive husband and Isabel said she came to look for work. Both women had lived in New York and had not previously had difficulty finding an apartment. Michelle left her apartment because of dangerous conditions, but thought she would be able to find another apartment. One mother, Sylvia, reported that she entered the shelter system because she thought it was the only way she would be able to get her own apartment. She was living with her grandmother and siblings and had been on a waiting list for a city-owned apartment for years.

Theme C: We Tried to Avoid Homelessness by Staying with Relatives, But It Was Tense and Uncomfortable.

Five of the six mothers turned to relatives when they were unable to find their own apartment. Relatives for these women were loosely defined and included the mothers of men they were involved with currently or in the past. The sixth mother, Sylvia, was already living doubled up in public housing with her grandmother and adult siblings. In all cases the situation became unbearable and the families entered the shelter system when they were either asked to leave or left of their own accord. In many cases the families they stayed with were already living in overcrowded conditions and the visiting family usually stayed on the living room floor. For example, Linda described what it was like when she stayed with her sister,

> She had her own husband and kids. So I didn't want to be a burden to them. She had three of her own plus my two. So it was five kids running all over the house and no place to go.

All of the mothers and eight of the fourteen children recalled tension and conflict while they lived with relatives. For example, Michelle and her five children tried to stay with the mother of the man with whom she was involved and with her grandmother. Neither situation worked for long because of arguments and lack of space. Evelyn and her two daughters first stayed in the basement of her brother's house but he threw them out after a short time. She then went to live with her youngest daughter's grandmother even though she was no longer involved with this woman's son. The family slept on the floor of this apartment but the arrangement failed quickly. Evelyn explained,

> We start staying with my daughter's grandmother, we get accused. She thought I was taking her money. But I told her son took it. I said your son took your money. Because he had put the blame for taking it on me.

Jimmy (age 11) recalled tension around money while he, his mother, and sister stayed with his aunt and uncle. He said, referring to his uncle,

> He would take money from my aunt from her purse because she was sleeping. And he would take the money and go to a job. And then when he comes home, he starts saying it was another person. Sometime he say it was my mother, sometime he it was the kids.

Elizabeth (age 10) refers to the man with whom her mother is involved as her stepfather. He is her brother's father and the family frequently stayed with this man's parents. She recalled fights over food:

> We used to live with my stepfather's family. And they used to say in the kitchen why they living with us, and my mother heard them and my mother got mad. And there was a big fight outside. Because my mother used to get her check and buy food. And my mother used to say don't take it because they always used to eat the food. They don't got no food. They always used to eat my mother's food. And my mother used to say come on, save it for the next meal. You know now they like my mother. They used to not talk no more after that fight. And then one of them says sorry to my mother.

CATEGORY II: EXPERIENCES IN THE SHELTER SYSTEM - PAST

Theme A: *It Was Traumatic to Live in the Hotels and Shelters.*

All the families spent some time in congregate shelters or welfare hotels before placement at the current shelter. The length of time spent in each type of shelter varied significantly. The Jones family spent two weeks in a barracks shelter before moving to the current placement and did not spend any time in a hotel. The Garcia family did not spend any time in a barracks shelter but was sent immediately to a hotel where they spent seven months. The

Michaels family spent one week in a barracks shelter before moving to a hotel where they stayed for four months before placement in the current shelter. All families reported traumatic events while living in these facilities.

Subtheme 1: We were living with a constant fear of danger. All mothers and seven children recalled feeling they were in danger while they lived in some shelters and hotels. This feeling of danger was particularly pervasive in the hotels. They recalled drugs, fires, break-ins, violence, and killings. The presence of drugs was particularly terrifying in the hotels. Isabel said that when she lived in the hotel, she saw drug dealers selling every kind of drug on the front steps of the hotel. Evelyn reported:

> When I first moved there the hotel had got busted because they were selling drugs in there. And the owner that owned the hotel when I first moved in, they took him too because he was selling drugs to people. He had a couple people selling drugs to the people in the rooms. And a lot of people got busted. Some got their kids took away from them.

Five of the children recalled that they heard or saw drug interactions while at the hotels. For example, Elizabeth (age 10) said "It was not too nice at the hotel. There were too many drugs. A lot of fighting over drugs."

In addition to drugs, participants reported other violent behavior. Evelyn, Dana and Cindy Smith said they were exposed to fires almost every night. For example, Dana (age 12) said:

> Night after night they would ring the fire bell and sometimes there's going to be a fire. And if my sister would be asleep, she'd jump up out of her sleep and start crying. And it scared her a lot. Some of the times we had a real big fire in there and everything. And we couldn't take that because my sister was scared. She got asthma and if she happened to have an asthma attack, we wouldn't have been able to get out of there because all that smoke would have been surrounding her and everything and it would have made it worse. So that's one of the main things we were scared about.

Although drug abuse was not so blatant in the shelters, Maria felt that much of the stealing she observed in the barracks shelter was drug related. She thought people would steal anything to get money for drugs and said:

> They were stealing high chairs. It's that drug, crack. Mess everything up. Because living in this situation, I know that a lot of homeless females be doing it. A lot. They stole from me. They took my iron. They stole a jacket I had, a long dungaree jacket.

Two families reported that people tried to break into their rooms at the hotels. For example, Linda said:

> The first day they actually tried to kick the door down because I guess somebody saw that I was in the shower or what not. And they tried kicking the door in to get inside. And my kids started screaming. Someone found out. And when I came out they said, your kids are downstairs because somebody tried to get into your room.

Although no one reported seeing any killings, several children and adults had heard about such events either from other people or on the news. For example, Maria said, "At the worst hotel there were a lot of killings, like in the hallway. Real bad." Her daughter, Annie (age 11) said about the same hotel, "It was not so good because people got shot. Not in the hallway but outside." Christina (age 11) who lived in a small hotel next to a larger one recalled events she heard about at the hotel next door. "They threw this baby out the window. And they used to kill there and everything. And there was a kid that got killed. . . And they killed this lady because that lady used all the money of selling drugs."

Subtheme 2: I felt dehumanized and mistreated by the people in charge. Families reported that they felt mistreated by the staff at the city's Emergency Assistance Units. Four of the six mothers said that they were sent from shelter to shelter when they first entered the system. They said that they were only allowed to stay for one night or sometimes not allowed to stay at all because the shelter or hotel did not expect them. For example, Christina (age 11) said,

> We went to the welfare and they sent us to this
> hotel. And when we went over there they said that
> they didn't know nothing about us so they sent us
> back.

In addition, participants reported that they often experienced
the strict rules and regulations imposed on them as a form of
mistreatment. Life in the shelters was very regimented. There were
curfews. Meals were served only at a certain time. Many mothers
and children viewed punishment for infractions of rules as severe.
For example, Elizabeth (age 10) said:

> They won't let you out. Only sometimes, you got
> to write your name when your going to go out on
> the paper. And they'll know who is out or in. And
> if you come in late, real late, the doors are closed
> and you be locked out. And they'll throw your
> things out and you won't be in the shelter no more.

Maria said that the workers in the hotels were not helpful when
she moved from one place to another . She said,

> You say, could you give me a van so I could take
> my things to the place I'm going. They say, no!
> You got to do it yourself. So I had to go by bus,
> subway, all the systems. And I just used to leave
> everything behind. So I lost a lot. A TV. A lot of
> stuff.

Subtheme 3: I felt isolated in the hotel. Some mothers and
children recalled feeling isolated in the hotel. They reported that
they were afraid to leave their rooms because of violent activity.
They also reported that they had no reason to leave the room
because of a lack of activities. Mothers and children spent much
time sitting in their room and watching television. Linda, who did
not have a television, recalled feeling bored because she had
nothing to do. Mothers tended to restrict their children to the room
because of the dangerous living conditions in the hotel. Children
reported feeling isolated because they had to stay in their rooms.
Annie (age 11) said:

> Some things I don't like about the hotel because
> it's boring. Like I don't get to go in the hallway. I

> gotta stay inside. . . It's too quiet. Nobody comes
> to my house. I don't get friends.

Dana (age 12) said:

> We realized that next door, they were selling drugs and
> everything and not only that. So we just stayed in our room half the
> time. If we're not in our room, then we'd be in Brooklyn at my
> aunt's house. It was hard because we was used to moving around
> and everything. Going outside, going places and stuff.

*Subtheme 4: Activities of daily living such as eating, sleeping and
bathing were stressful in the shelters and hotels.* Eating was a
difficult proposition in the shelters and hotels. In the shelters,
families were expected to eat all their meals in the on-site
cafeteria. Almost all the children who spent time in these shelters
disliked the food. For example, Elizabeth (age 10) said:

> I used to not like it because they used to feed you
> food. They used to make you eat. You got to go to
> a little cafeteria and everyone eats. They used to
> give nasty food. They give breakfast, lunch and
> dinner. If you don't wake up early you can't eat.
> Then you be starved.

One mother, Sylvia, thought the food made her children sick.
She said:

> It was like TV food. And every time they start
> eating it, after the first week, they got sick. They
> keep vomiting and vomiting. And they kept giving
> them medicine for it and they wouldn't stop. So
> then I started taking them to restaurants. And they
> was alright then. They didn't get sick no more. So
> I figure it was the shelter's food.

In the hotels, all families set up makeshift kitchens with hot
plates and small refrigerators. However, in most cases such
arrangements were against the hotel regulations and families risked
eviction if they were discovered. For example, Christina (age 11)
said:

> We couldn't bring no stove in there, no
> refrigerators or nothing. . . My mother sneaked in
> this little refrigerator. And when there was
> inspection, she put a tablecloth on and made
> believe it was a little table.

Sleeping was also problematic. In the hotels, it was typical for family members to have to share beds. Three mothers and three children recalled overcrowded conditions in the hotels and shelters. For example, Jose (age 13) said:

> It was uncomfortable. It was crowded. I used to
> have to sleep with my sister. Sometimes I didn't
> sleep with her.. I slept on a hard mattress my
> mother put on the floor. It would be better living in
> the street. You got more room.

In the barracks shelters, the lack of privacy was a source of stress and discomfort for the families. Families slept in a large room with many beds, and many found it difficult to live in such close proximity. For example, Sylvia said,

> No privacy. It was weird because I wasn't used to
> living around people. You couldn't get comfortable
> like you would do at your own house. . . Sometime
> I didn't sleep. I stayed up because it's
> uncomfortable when you have to watch children.
> Because they had women there with their men and
> all of that. So you had to keep your eyes open.

In addition, mothers and children reported that the shelters were unclean. Robert (age 9) said he saw "the rats going in people's food and sneaking in people's stuff when they be sleep." He said that he slept with the covers over his head so that the rats could not bother him. Maria said, "It was disgusting. I mean, real filthy and all the bathrooms dirty, everything dirty." Linda stated that it was hard for her to take a shower at the hotel because the shower was not in the room. She had to leave her eleven year old son and three year old daughter alone in the room when she bathed. On one occasion, she said that someone tried to break into her room while she was bathing.

Theme C: I Liked the Shelters and Hotels Where We Stayed.

Several children recalled positive experiences in some of the hotels and shelters. Four of the children said they enjoyed living in the hotels. Generally, the children liked smaller and safer hotels. Children seemed to enjoy hotels where it was easy for them to meet other people and make friends. For example, Jimmy (age 11) met a friend he played with after school. He said that they used to go to the park near the hotel and play tag. Another child, Jose (age 13), joined a group of children who banded together in the hotel and seemed to engage in dangerous activities such as riding on top of the elevator and breaking into hotel rooms. He said that he had a good time at the hotel. Two sisters, Annie (age 11) and Elizabeth (age 10), who lived in several hotels liked one of them because they had many friends and liked the school they attended. Three siblings, John (age 11), Robert (age 9) and Julissa (age 7), liked the hotel they stayed in very much. They had friends and enjoyed the proximity of the hotel to the beach. The family felt comfortable in two rooms and Robert said, "It was like a home."

In general, the mothers were less positive about the hotels and shelters than the children. However, Michelle liked the hotel her family was placed in. She said,

> It was nice I liked it. If we had to stay there I would have stayed because it didn't cause no problems. I didn't have any. If you didn't want to be bothered with nobody you just stayed in your room and nobody be messing with you. It was like a big private house. Real big. I think it was like three stories and they only had one apartment and two rooms on every floor. If you wanted to go out the managers would watch the children, they would make sure nothing would go wrong. That's the type of people they were. They didn't have to be like that.

Six children liked the shelter environment where could easily meet many friends. Annie (age 11) described this experience best. She said,

> It was warm. Because I used to know everybody. Everybody in there was my friend. It's fun because it feels so exciting. And my mother has a lot of friends.

None of the mothers liked the congregate shelter environment with the exception of Maria who liked it the first time she was sent but not the second. She said, "the first time I went to the shelter it was great. I got along with everybody. But the second time I went it was disgusting. Real filthy."

CATEGORY III: EXPERIENCES IN THE SHELTER SYSTEM - PRESENT

Theme A: *I Feel Much More Secure Because I Know I Can Stay Here Until I Find an Apartment.*

Almost all the mothers stated that they felt better knowing that this shelter was the last one they would have to live in. They seemed able to relax with the knowledge that they would be moving to an apartment after this placement. For example, Maria said, "You see like you have hope here that it's going to get better. It's not going to get no worse."

Subtheme 1: I wish I could stay here forever. All the families had been placed in this shelter for a number of months and were generally very happy there. Many of the mothers and children expressed the wish that they could stay in the shelter instead of moving elsewhere. The knowledge that they would have to leave caused some anxiety, particularly in the children. For example, Christina (age 11) said:

> Because I love my house and every day I think now I'm in this school and then when we get the apartment, I'm going to have to change to this other school and I'm going to have to meet other friends. I want my permanent house. Only if here could be your permanent house, I would stay here. I would.

Theme B: *We Feel Safe Here.*

Mothers repeatedly stated that they felt safe in this shelter. For example, Maria said,

> You don't see no drugs. That's my main prerogative. You could walk the hallways at five

in the morning. Just because the workers aren't here you don't see no dealing.

Linda said,

And there's a lot of security. There's a lot of people helping out. Like right now we have social workers here nine to five. We have guards during the night who have certain hours that they're in case of any emergency.

Many of the children also seemed to feel safe. I observed that they played freely in front of the shelter and in the schoolyard next door. Parents could often watch their children from the window of their apartment.

Theme C: We Have Almost Everything We Need Here.

Mothers and children were very happy with the facilities at the current shelter where they were housed in small apartments. For example, Linda said:

When I came in here, I actually cried when I saw it was so big and roomy. I said, but this is like my own apartment. It's so beautiful. And I really liked it when I came in. They supplied us right away with the dishes and everything we needed. It was something you don't see in most shelters. If they give you a towel and soap, that's enough.

Sylvia said that she and her children were much happier in the current shelter than they were in the barracks shelter. She said, "This is like a home. They have they own private house." Annie (age 11) said she liked this shelter better than the other places because she has her own room. Robert (age 9) said that he liked the current shelter because "this ain't no little room here and we got enough rooms for me to sleep."

Theme D: I've Never Had So Many Opportunities In My Life.

All of the mothers stated that they participated in many of the activities available at this shelter. The activities mentioned include support groups, educational groups, educational opportunities and job training. For children the shelter provides a preschool, recreational programs and a summer day camp.

Subtheme 1: The groups and meetings they have at this shelter are very helpful. All the mothers said that they participated in the groups and meetings available at the shelter to some extent. Weekly groups focused on various topics such as coping, self help, and parenting. For example, Maria said:

> Almost every day there's a meeting. You don't have to participate but it's there to help you move. The meetings are very useful especially the coping meeting. . . You express your feelings, tell them how you feel about living here. It's like having friends and you don't feel so alone.

Isabel explained how she benefits from her participation in the coping group:

> It's like how you feel, if you feel anger, what you're going to do. So we write down what we feel and everything and then we discuss. . . If you feel sorrow, anger like that. It's nice. For me it's like counseling, too. Because at the same time, you be in your house just thinking by yourself and all those things make you explode more fast. Now when you go to some places like that you can share your emotions and it can help you.

Linda was also very positive about the meetings. She said:

> They have self-help programs where they help you with your budgeting, your status here, welfare problems. Any sort of problems. We have meetings for all sorts of things. They are very helpful. They help me like we have on they call the parenting group. . . And it's helped me a lot especially with my daughter because she's a bit hyper, she's hyperactive.

Subtheme 2: I feel my social worker cares about me and my family and helps us in many ways. All but one of the mothers felt that their social workers at the shelter helped them in various ways.

Almost all mentioned receiving help in obtaining an apartment. They stated that they were helped with an application for public housing almost as soon as they arrived. Some women seemed to engage in a counseling relationship with their worker who helped them with emotional difficulties as well as with more concrete services. For example, Maria said:

> The worker I got here is great. He gets involved. He speaks to my daughters. Let's say in the beginning, my daughters felt left out because of my son's father or whatever. And they wouldn't tell me but they told him. And if they have a party or they giving away something, he real quick puts it in my mailbox. Like they're giving out turkey, Maria on so and so day. He finds out and real quick he tells me.

Two women also stated that the social workers and other staff at the shelter were helpful and would mediate disputes between them and other people at the shelter.

Subtheme 3: My social worker doesn't support me or respect my privacy. Only one mother, Evelyn, had anything negative to say about the social work staff at the shelter. She felt that her worker did not take her side when she had difficulty with other women at the shelter and was too "nosy" in their sessions.

Subtheme 4: The programs and activities for children at the shelter are good. Mothers mentioned that their children participated in organized activities at the shelter. For example, the center had its own child care center for preschool children. Linda, who has a 3 year old daughter felt this school was a very positive experience for her child. She said,

> The teachers love her. And they were so excited about how fast she learned. The promoted her to a higher class because she's so smart. For a child who came from Puerto Rico you would think that she had difficulty learning the language right away. And she's learning so quick, you can't get her to speak anything else now.

In addition, mothers and children reported that the shelter provided a day camp for children in the summer and a recreation program during the year on Saturdays. Most of the children attended the programs. Linda spoke highly of the recreational programs that her eleven year old son attends at the shelter. She said,

> The kids have a lot of activities. They had day camp. They would go out almost every single day. They go to the movies and they go to other places too.

Jose (age 13) said that he had mixed feelings about the summer camp, but did attend. He said,

> They treat us like little kids. They treat us like five, six years old. I didn't like it because it was boring. I went for two or three months. They took us to Bear Mountain. They took us to seven lakes. They took us to the zoo. They take us to the movies and to the museum.

Jose said that he attends the recreational programs on Saturdays depending on where the group is going. He said he goes when, "they take us to around to basketball games, skating, museums, places like that."

CATEGORY IV: EMOTIONAL CONSEQUENCES

Theme A: I Felt Anxious
Three of six mothers reported that they felt anxious because they did not know what would happen to their family. They imagined a terrible future. For example, Maria said:

> It was a strange feeling, every day. What's going to happen the next day. But at the beginning it was hard. Not knowing where I was going to sleep the next day.

Linda expressed a similar feeling. She said:

> When I was in the hotel I didn't know what would happen from the hotel to here and everything. You

know, was I going to be that long in the hotel?
Would something happen to me or the kids?
Would I be able to handle all the changes? I used
to worry about everything.

Three children expressed anxiety related to the uncertainty
about their situation. Annie explained her feelings:

It was hard because I had to meet a lot of friends,
to get used to the place. I was scared. You know,
the teachers I didn't know how they would treat
me. And going to a lot of schools and see what's
next and what's next, and then I might leave my
book in the desk and then I got to leave to another
shelter and I might leave my book. Or I might
leave something personal. Like my ring, forget it.
It probably fell there. And I remembered that it
fell there. And then I forget about it like. That's
why I used to be scared.

Jennifer (age 13) said, "All the times I left a place I felt
nauseous when I was leaving. When I move I get used to it."

Theme B: I Felt Depressed

Three mothers admitted to feeling depressed by their
experiences and situation. Maria said, "I used to cry a lot." Linda
stated, "I would get depressed enough, I would go lock myself in my
room and cry."

Subtheme 1: I felt hopeless. Isabel revealed her feelings of
hopelessness when she discussed her self-destructive behavior and
suicidal thoughts.

I almost destroyed myself too, because I started
drinking. . . I'd see my kids, look at where they're
coming, what you coming here for, I would cry,
just cry. I can't take it. I can't live here in the
hotel, I can't, I can't. I don't know what I'm going
to do one of these days. Sometimes I think stupid
things, I think I'm going to kill myself. Because I
can't take it, I can't be living in that insanity.

Subtheme 2: I felt sad because I lost so much. All families had to cope with many losses since they became homeless. Different participants felt sad about different things. Many children stated that they felt sad when they had to leave a school they liked. For example, Jimmy (age 11) said:

> At the hotel I went to another school for a month. It was good. My teacher was good too. . . I felt sad when I left. Only once I got to go to go on a trip over there. . . I didn't want to go to a new school. I wanted to come there. But the bus from here, it don't take me there.

Elizabeth (age 10) expressed similar feelings:

> And I liked a lot of people there. They were nice. That was my favorite school. No fights at all. And I always used to have friends. We always used to play together. And I used to go to after school, they used to help me with my home work. And when we used to finish, we used to paint, do something, make ourselves something to eat. I felt sad when I left that school. I mean, I started crying to my mother. I said, "Ma, I don't want leave this school." She says, "Well, we have to because we're moving." And then we moved and we came to another — a shelter. Then we got here.

Alison, Diana and Jason Jones desperately missed their great-grandmother with whom they had lived. Alison and Jason cried when they talked about her. Alison (age 8) said:

> I wanted to live with my grandmother. When my mother leaves, I stay with her. I wanted to stay with my grandmother because she gave me more than my mother gave me. I was crying.

Annie (age 11), who had been in and out of the shelter system for three years, described how she felt about losing many of her possessions:

I don't like to lose things. I lost a lot. Like clothes, like dresses. Little bitty things like one doll. But one doll is a lot to me. We lost a lot, though. That was the problem. Because they would keep it in a stall. My mother would tell them to keep it there in a basement or something. And they say you got up to a week. And my mother wouldn't make it that week. It would be theirs. They wouldn't give it back. So that was the problem. I miss a lot of it. Right now this whole room would be piled up.

Subtheme 3: I'm ashamed to be homeless. The intense feeling of shame was articulated by one child. Jennifer (age 13) said, "Nobody knows I'm out here in the shelter except for my godfather, my grandmother and my uncles. My friends don't." She added:

I like this place but it's the name shelter I don't like. It's called a shelter for the homeless. Homeless means people that don't have places to go. No food. We have all of it. If you got it then why you want to be called homeless.

Theme C: I Felt Angry

Two of the women acknowledged feelings of anger at their predicament. Both felt that they were victimized by unscrupulous landlords. For example, Evelyn thought she was evicted because her landlord did not like her. She said, "The landlord told me she wanted the apartment for her family. But she didn't want it for her family. She rented it out to somebody else." Evelyn reported that she was angry because she was unable to prevent the eviction.

Many children reported that they were teased at school because they live in a shelter. Almost all of the children reported being referred to as "castle" children. The neighborhood children have devised this name because of the shape of the shelter building. For example, Christina (age 11) said:

My friends, some of them say, I'm never going to live in a shelter. I don't like to live in a shelter. Like that. And they said that, they don't like shelters or nothing. They never come and live in it. And I feel bad. Because, just because I live in a shelter doesn't mean I ain't not being different.

There's nothing different between us. We human,
right? It doesn't matter. Because for me, I don't
care if I have a friend that she's blue, purple, pink,
whatever color. Brown, black, I don't care. I still
like them.

Alison (age 8) and her sister, Jackie (age 6) said that they are
frequently teased in school. Jackie said "they say we live in a
castle. And they say we poor and we can't dress." Alison said,
"Only the people that don't live here, they tease us. They say that's
why you live in the Castle, and that's why you poor. . . don't like
when people call me poor."

Theme D: My Health Suffered
Several participants reported that the stress of homelessness
exacerbated existing health problems. Isabel suffered from asthma,
back pains, and migraine headaches. Cindy had asthma. Evelyn
was a diabetic. Dana reported backaches. Isabel described her
back difficulties:

When I became homeless the first time. That was
a disaster for me. I had a breakdown. I have a bad
breakdown. And then it comes so that I can't not
even move my back, my back pains. That was the
first time. But now I try to calm down, go outside,
take a walk, like that, so I don't break down like
that.

Dana (age 12) worried about her sister who has asthma and her
mother who is diabetic. She said,

I worry about my sister, because every time
something happen, she'd get scared and she would
start crying and then she might start wheezing. I
worry about her and my mother because my mother
is also sick and with everything that go on around
here where people saying she do all these things, it
makes her mad. And when she get mad, it's like
it's making her sickness get worse.

Theme E: I Felt Relieved and Hopeful

Two of the mothers mentioned that they did not feel as if they were homeless after they were placed in the Tier II shelter. Sylvia said:

> Being homeless, that's the worst thing in the world. But now I say I'm a rich woman. I live in a castle. Okay they call this place the castle. From the school, the neighbors, the kids say oh, you live in the castle. You know what I mean when I say castle. But when I see those people in the park, all those people they're living on the ground, they ain't got no real place to live. And I say God, I'm rich. At least I have food, a place, something, a bed, a roof to sleep. But those people are living on the street.

Michelle said:

> I mean I respect myself more. I feel much better about myself. At one time I wanted to put the kids away and go lock myself in a hospital some place because I felt I couldn't take it no more. Since I been here it hasn't bothered me. It's like I'm more prepared to deal with them now and life too. I'm more content and ready.

Three of the mothers reported feeling good about their participation in classes offered at the shelter. in order to prepare for their high school equivalency exam. For example, Maria described her preparation for the high school equivalency exam:

> I'm registered here, going to school with this lady. She gives classes to us.. She helps us with math, reading, science, everything. She's like a teacher to us. It's so that I will have high school equivalency. . . It's like triple the time you would do in a regular school. But it's something. I got to eleventh grade before.

Four of the mothers reported that they felt good about being able to work and to get some job training for the future. Isabel was enrolled in an organized job training program at the shelter. She said:

> It's nice, I like it. And when I move out of here, they going to find me good work, a good job, maybe in word processing because I have some skill on the computer.

CATEGORY V: IMPACT ON RELATIONSHIPS

Theme A: Being Homeless Made it Difficult to Maintain Relationships.

Families who had relatives living in the metropolitan area reported that they were placed in shelters far from their old neighborhood. Most families managed to make the trip when they wanted to visit. However, Maria recalls one placement on Staten Island where it was very difficult to visit her mother or other relatives.

Subtheme 1: I had to hide my relationship with the man with whom I'm involved. Some shelters or hotels had strict rules about visitors which made it difficult for women to maintain relationships with men. However, the current shelter allowed women to have visitors as often as they chose. Five of the mothers had ongoing relationships with men who stayed with them at times.

Theme B: Parenting In the Shelter Environment Has Been Challenging.

Many parents recalled difficulties associated with parenting. They found the hotels and congregate shelters particularly hard places to rear children.

Subtheme 1: My child's behavior seemed to deteriorate after we became homeless. Four of six mothers felt that their children's behavior changed in some way after they became homeless. Two mothers reported increased aggressive behavior in their sons. Isabel, the mother of Jose (age 13) placed him in foster care while they lived in a hotel because his behavior was so unmanageable. Sylvia, Jason's (age 5) mother found that her son continued to behave appropriately at home but had become aggressive in school after they moved to the shelter. Linda felt her son Jimmy (age 11) was depressed after they entered the shelter system. He would not do his work in class. He was very unhappy particularly when he had to switch schools for the third time in one year. Maria felt that her daughter Emily (age 11) had become more moody and irritable since they became homeless.

Subtheme 2: I try to protect my children from the horror and danger associated with shelter life. All the mothers tried to protect their children from danger by watching them very carefully. They also frequently restricted them to the room or apartment. For example, Maria would let her daughters visit their friends in the shelter but would not let them take their coats so she could be sure they would not go outside since it was winter.

Subtheme 3: I feel guilty and inadequate as a parent for exposing my children to this. Two of the mothers expressed feelings of guilt about exposing their children to shelter and hotel life. For example, Isabel said that she felt terrible when she saw her children come back to the hotel from school. Maria said, "Being homeless is a terrible feeling especially if you got children." She described how she felt while staying in one of the hotels:

> For me it wasn't that bad because I used to stay indoors. But for the kids when they used to come from school, they used to see all the transactions in the elevators. It was real ugly."

Theme C: It Was Difficult to Make New Friends.

Many of the children stated that the hardest thing about going to a new school was meeting new friends. For example, Jimmy (age 11) said, "It was a little bit hard when I went to a new school because then I had to make new friends and then, and that was awful." Annie (age 11) said, "I didn't meet so many friends because I'm so quiet." Jose (age 13) said:

> The hardest thing for me is making friends. That's all. It's hard for me, making new friends moving from one place to another and having to make new friends.

CATEGORY VI: ACADEMIC CONSEQUENCES

Theme A: Homelessness Had a Negative Impact On My Children's Education.

Four of six mothers felt that becoming homeless had some negative impact on their children's education. For example, Maria said:

> They left back and everything. Annie's in fourth.
> She belongs in sixth. Elizabeth's in third. She
> belongs in fifth. And it all has to do with moving
> around so much. I know they're not that smart but
> they're not stupid at all.

However, not all the children were left back a grade because of their difficulty. Jimmy's mother noticed that he was having trouble in school and talked to the principal and teacher. He was transferred to an English as a Second Language class where he started to do better. Evelyn felt that her daughter, Dana (age 12), missed a lot of school when they moved because she had to travel such a long distance to return to her old school. According to her mother, Dana continues to miss school because of chronic back pain. Sylvia feels her children's education was compromised when she transferred them to the school near the shelter which she feels is inferior to the school they were attending in her old neighborhood.

Theme B: I Hated Changing Schools So Often.

All the children changed schools at least once after their family entered the shelter system. Most children changed schools more than once within a year. Many of the children also missed school when they moved from place to place.

Subtheme 1: I love the school I go to now and don't want to change again. Christina (age 11) said:

> I like this school a lot and that's why I tell my
> mother when we move, I want her to move around
> here. And I told her that if we move far away, I
> want to take a bus, a school bus or anything
> because I want to come here back to this school
> until I pass.

Subtheme 2: I liked my old school better than this one and wish I could have stayed there. Alison (age 8) said:

> I didn't want to go to this school. I didn't like it. I wanted to stay at my other school but my mother said, no. You don't learn a lot from these people. When they teach they don't teach us right like they teach us over there. Over here they punch and curse at the teacher and the teachers don't do nothing. And my other principal used to do stuff.

Subtheme 3: It seemed like I was always behind and trying to catch up with the rest of the class. Children were often required to switch schools in the middle of the school year which made it difficult for them to keep up with the class. In addition, some children missed a lot of school when the family moved. For example, Annie (age 11) presented the child's point of view regarding this situation:

> It was hard moving to so many schools. That was hard. Because I used to leave there and then I probably miss the test and I had to go to another one and catch up with them. Catch up, that was hard, too. I'm supposed to be in the sixth going into seventh. So many schools I had to switch. I didn't know what was next so I missed a lot of things. Sometimes I wasn't in school. You know, I missed a lot of days because we had to do this, fix up this, put this in another spot. You know, take all those bags and unload them like that. Half and half. Half and half.

Subtheme 4: Sometimes I was just too tired to pay attention to what was going on in school. Elizabeth (age 10) recalled being too tired to pay attention in class at times:

> We used to move a lot and I used to be tired. And we always used to move in the night sometimes because the van used to be late. We always used to move around in a van, a different van. And it used to come late sometimes and I used to be sleepy and then my mother have to wake me up and I'd be tired. In school the next day the teacher

used to say, have you slept and I'd say, no. And
she used to say if you're sleepy, go in the back and
lay down, put your head down. And I would go in
the back and lay down sometimes.

Alison (age 8) also recalled being tired in school when she
lived in a shelter. She said, "I always used to stay up. I used to be
dreaming but not very good dreams. . . about monsters and
everything."

CATEGORY VII. SUPPORTS

Theme A: My Family Is Supportive and Helpful.
All the families seemed to be very close and to spend much
time together. Mothers seemed to rely on their children for help and
support and children seemed to depend on their mothers and
siblings. Many participants considered their extended family as an
additional source of support.

Subtheme 1: My child is a source of support and help. Four
mothers relied on their older children to watch the younger ones.
For example, Evelyn's twelve year old daughter, Dana picked up
her six year old sister, Cindy, after school and watched her in the
afternoon while Evelyn attended school. Jimmy (age 11) watched
his three year old sister when his mother worked for a few hours at
the shelter.

*Subtheme 2: My mother is the most important person in the world
to me.* Twelve of the children said that their mother helps them
when things get hard. For example, Jose (age 13) said, "My mom.
That's the only person that tries to help me a lot. She gives advice
and she talks to me a lot." Annie (age 11) said:

My mother helps me when things are hard. She be
with me all the way. She never left me. She be
there all through everything when I needed her,
when I needed to cry over my things. I needed
somebody to lean on and I had my mother to lean
on.

Alison (age 8) said:

> My mother tells me more interesting things than
> my brother and sisters because I understands it.
> And I tell her because sometimes she understands.
> I don't think my sister and brother understand.

Subtheme 3: Relatives have helped us through this experience.
Five of the six families had extended family who lived in the
metropolitan area. Most families visited these relatives who helped
in many ways. Six children said that they liked visiting their
relatives which included fathers, grandparents, aunts, uncles and
cousins. For example, Dana (age 12) said:

> My aunt mostly helps us because when we had
> problems, we would go to her with them, she
> would help us out and everything. And some of the
> nights when we didn't want to come back home,
> she would let us stay there. She helped us with a
> lot. She looks for apartments for my mother and
> everything.

Jennifer (age 13) said that she often rides the subway to visit
relatives, "I visit my godfather, my uncle, my father, my
stepmother, my godmother, my grandmother. They give me
money."

*Subtheme 4: I'm disappointed that my family has not been helpful
or supportive enough.* Michelle expressed the feeling that her family
did not help or support her enough when she became homeless. She
said that she once let her uncle live with her when he had no where
to stay but when she wanted to stay with him he refused to have her.
She really cannot understand how her grandmother who raised her
can turn her away knowing that her great grandchildren are
involved. On occasion she has dropped the children off and left to
stay elsewhere because she knew her grandmother would not turn
them away if she was not there.

Theme B: Men Help Financially and Emotionally but They're Unreliable.

Five of six mothers were involved in a relationship with a man
at the time of the study. Two of the women seemed to be living
with men. They all said that the men they were involved with
helped them on occasion. The men helped financially, provided
emotional support, and helped with the children. For example,

Maria had been in a relationship with her son's father for four years. However, she said:

> He just started this job, construction. That's not all
> the time he has work. Because I would have had
> an apartment and all that. But now he is. I don't
> know how long that will last. And I don't count on
> it neither. If he gives his son fine but I don't count
> on it.

Sylvia said about the father of her unborn child,

He works. At times he gives me money. I really don't ask him because he has his own family to deal with. But he gives me. And he has rent to pay where he lives at. But when he gives, I take it.

She said that he also helps her watch the children sometimes. She said, "He keeps them sometimes but I don't want to force nothing on him." Michelle enjoys spending time with the man she's involved with. She said:

> Like my friend he come. You know and we sit and
> watch TV, listen to music, we play cards and I'm
> content now. Yes and I wanted to marry him
> because me and him understood each other. We
> could sit down and talk about anything without
> arguing or fighting. Sometimes we have little
> disagreements but I understand him and he
> understand me. He know he could tell me
> anything and I could tell him anything. Like with
> him he tell me you could go out for a little while
> by yourself. You deserve a little free time for
> yourself because I'm always constantly doing
> something for the children, keeping the house
> clean.

Theme C: I Have Friends Who Help Me.

Most of the mothers developed friendships with other women while living in the current shelter and had at least one friend in the shelter. For example, Maria said:

> There's a lot of good people here and when new
> people come, that's the first thing I tell them. And

> I tell them also where I live and any time you need
> anything, knock on my door.

Isabel developed a friendship with another women at the shelter who already moved out. They still visit each other and her friend gives her advice based on her own experience. In addition to social companionship, friends often give these women useful information. For example, Evelyn learned from a friend that she could get a telephone installed for medical reasons since her daughter has asthma. Michelle relies on her neighbors for loans of money when she runs out of food or another essential item. However, she said that she realizes the drawbacks of this strategy and is trying to stop. She said,

> Sometimes I borrow and sometimes I just try to
> hold out until I get my check so this way I don't
> have to pay nobody back. Like I said I have other
> things to do so if I have to pay somebody back I
> have to slack off on something else. Like I can't
> get them something or get me something I can't do
> that or buy extra food. I couldn't do that if I be
> borrowing. I used to borrow a lot. I really pulled
> myself down from doing that cause it wasn't paying
> off. Every time I got more money I had to do
> things plus pay people back. I had nothing for
> myself. I end up still paying you back and saying
> if you really don't need it can I borrow it back until
> my next check.

Sylvia said she does not have any real friends in the shelter and that her best girlfriend lives in her old neighborhood. Sylvia visits her frequently and usually sleeps at her apartment on the weekends. Her friend has helped her since she left her apartment. For instance, when she used to bring her children to school in their old neighborhood she would spend the day with her friend until it was time to pick the children up from school
Most of the children said that they had friends who lived in the shelter or in the projects across the street. Most children described enjoyable experiences playing with their friends. The two older boys, Jose (age 13) and Jimmy (age 11) said they enjoyed playing ball outside with their friends. For example, Jimmy said:

> Sometimes we go to the park over there to play
> baseball. . . I like football too. Sometimes I go
> outside from morning to afternoon.

Jose has a best friend who is nineteen and lives in the housing
projects. He said that he doesn't like children his age. The sisters,
Annie (age 10) and Elizabeth (age 11), have best friends who are
also sisters. They play with them whenever they are not in school.
Dana (age 12) and Christina (age 11) said that most of their friends
had moved away already. They seemed to spend most of their time
in the shelter alone or with their family. However, Christina said
that she has a best friend in school and had a best friend who lived
in the shelter whom she frequently visits on the weekend. Alison
(age 8) said that her friends help her because, "They tell me more
things that I never know. Like about friends and sometimes they
tell me what to do and what not to do." Jennifer (age 13) said that
her boyfriend helps her and other members of her family. She said:

> He play with us. He bring games over for us to
> play. He help my brothers with their homework.
> He help all of us. He help my mother. My mother
> ask him to clean the house he do it. If he got
> money he'll give my mother and then my mother
> will pay him back the next day he come over.

The younger children seemed to spend most of their time
with their family and to play primarily with siblings or
cousins when not in school.

Theme D: I'm Wary About Getting Too Involved With The Other Residents.

While most women felt that the other residents were friendly
and supportive, two of the mothers described conflict with some of
the other women in the shelter. They both described incidents where
other women tried to get them in trouble for things they didn't do.
Evelyn, said that she was frequently accused of starting fights when
she wasn't even at the shelter because she was at school. Maria said
she had been reported to child welfare by one of her neighbors who
accused her of drug abuse and child abuse. When the claim was
investigated she was cleared. However, she described a group of
women who are living at the shelter and abusing drugs. She feels
these women bother other women for food and money after they
spend all their money on drugs. Maria feels these women called

child welfare because she had refused to give them money on several occasions.

Theme E: I Get Help From Organizations in the Community.

Seven of the fourteen children attended an after school program. The program was held four days per week and provided homework help, recreation and dinner. The children all seemed to like the program and the mothers seemed to appreciate the help with child care. For example, Alison (age 8) said "I like it because it's like different teachers that you meet that I don't know when I go to regular school. And I meet new friends."

Two of the six mothers seemed to reach beyond the shelter to other organizations for help. Linda took her children to several organizations that gave out toys for the holidays. She sent her son to a Sunday school run by a neighborhood church. Isabel was the only one who contacted advocacy groups for the homeless who were helping her find an apartment in a building under rehabilitation. She also used an Hispanic counseling center and attended a support group there until she started her job at the shelter.

CATEGORY VIII: COPING STRATEGIES

Theme A: I've Learned To Use the System To My Advantage.

Many of the mothers became quite knowledgeable about the rules and regulations of the welfare and shelter systems. For example, they said that they learned what to do to get their family placed in a better living situation such as the current shelter. These strategies seemed to be a combination of their knowledge about their rights and the different types of shelter available. In addition, several mothers felt that good behavior and getting to know the workers in the shelters would be rewarded with a better placement.

Subtheme 1: I've learned to be my own advocate. All of the mothers described some instances of when they were able to help improve their situation. Evelyn explained how she managed to get transferred from a welfare hotel to the current shelter by refusing to accept placements she did not want. She said:

> I just went downstairs and told my crisis worker
> they had to find me somewhere else to go because

I couldn't take it there no more. The first day they
found me a place to go, they just put me in another
hotel near the airport. And I told her I didn't want
to go to another hotel because it was too far. So I
turned that down. Then they wanted to send me to
a shelter in another neighborhood. And I told her I
didn't want to go there because I don't know
nothing about that neighborhood. The next day I
went downstairs he gave me the book, told me to
pick any place I wanted to pick so I picked here.

Maria thought she was able to get transferred from the barracks
shelter to a better placement by complaining. She said:

I just complained, keep on giving complaints. Get
me out of here and I don't want to go to no terrible
hotel. If you're going to put me in a bad place,
leave me here.

Sylvia said all her children are in the right grades because:

I made sure of that. Because at first they wanted
to put them in different grades. They were saying
my daughter was in Kindergarten and my other
daughter was in second grade. I said, No, they just
graduated from Kindergarten and second grade. I
had to get they report cards to prove it to them so
they could get in the right grades. Lucky I had
them.

*Subtheme 2: Entering the shelter system was my strategy for
getting an apartment.* Two of the mothers said that they had filled
out applications for city housing many years ago but were never
contacted until they moved to the shelter. Sylvia said,

I had an application in for city housing for almost
five years. And they never called me. I just had
an interview since I lived here but before they ain't
never called me for housing.

Theme B: *I Try to Avoid Problems By Staying Alone or With My Family.*

This was the most commonly used coping strategy. Maria explained how she used this strategy while living in the shelter:

> I just stay away from the other residents and go watch TV. My kids used to go to school and I would go in the TV room, smoke my cigarettes, watch TV. When the kids used to come home we used to leave. There was a park across the street. . . And we used to go to the park and stay there until late. Have a picnic everyday. So we wasn't stuck in there. People would say, "Where were you?" "Why do you do that?" I said just not to be in here. Be on my own with my kids. Because we don't want to be around bad. So we just stay away from it.

Evelyn relied on this strategy while she lived in a hotel and continues to use it in the current shelter. She said at the hotel "most of the people was on drugs so I just stayed in my room." In the current shelter she said that since she has been blamed for starting trouble with other residents "Now I stay to myself. I stays upstairs." Jennifer (age 13) said:

> After school I come upstairs. I don't go outside. I just stay in the house and play cards with my friend. We have money and we bring in stuff to eat. We play cards. We look at TV. We do math. We do spelling. I don't go outside because there's trouble. Girls start with you. You get in the wrong crowd. So I don't go outside.

Michelle said:

> I don't hang out around here no more. Like the people in the office, they've seen me so they know me and they told me. In the beginning the lady told me just don't hang out with the wrong people. And it seems like that's just what I went for, the wrong ones. You know and I had to go off out here and stuff like that. You know but they didn't write me up or anything because they knew I stayed to

myself. And these people would come up to me. I would be outside sitting by myself on the car and they'll walk up to me volunteering information that I didn't even ask and then turn around later. . . Three girls wanted to fight me one night just because I didn't want to say hello to one of them. And I thought that was really stupid.

Theme C: Sometimes I Need a Drink to Calm Myself.

Isabel and Michelle reported drinking on a regular basis. Isabel said that she drank frequently when she lived in the hotel because of the stress. However, said she drinks much less now. She said, "I don't tell you that I stopped drinking but like that time it was every day. And now every two weeks and not too much." Michelle also said that she drinks less now then she previously. She said, "sometimes I need a drink. The pressure gets to me. I don't want to go crazy. Not until I raise them up anyway."

Theme D: I Keep Busy So That I Don't Think About My Situation Too Much.

Most of the older girls spent their time after school and on weekends in the apartment. For instance, Dana (age 12) said:

> After school, I just come upstairs, clean up what I have to clean upstairs. Got to do my homework. If I don't go to sleep, I watch TV. And that's it.

Christina (age 11) said after school "I stay here. Watch TV. See cartoons. See games. Play Nintendo." The mothers often joined their children in these activities.

The boys seemed to spend most of their time outdoors playing sports such as football and basketball. Jose (age 13) said that he is hardly ever home after school. He said, "I go outside with my friends we play football everyday." John (age 11) and Robert (age 9) said that they spent most of their time after school and on weekends playing basketball and baseball. Jimmy (age 11) also played baseball and played outside whenever he had time. One of the girls, Julissa (age 7) also liked to play outside. She said, "I ask my mother could I go outside? Could I take out my bike? She says, yeah and I ride some of my friends on it."

Theme E: I'm Always Ready To Defend My Integrity.

Many of the children said that they fight with other children when they are hit first or insulted, or if either of these things happen to someone in their family. Jason (age 5) said:

> I be mad when they be beating up my sister. I hit them back. My friends help me fight too. They say curses, they say the letter A word, they talking bad about my mother. They say F your house.

Jennifer (age 13) said, "I just stay upstairs cause I'm tough. If somebody messes with my brothers or they say something about my mother I'll fight them."

Theme F: I Make New Friends As Quickly As I Can.

Many of the children seemed to make new friends quickly when they entered a shelter or hotel. Julissa (age 7) explained what it was like when she moved to a new place. She said,

> You're not gonna have no friends to play with. You're gonna be alone by yourself. And you only gonna see some friends be with the other friends. That won't help you make friends if you won't go over there and ask them could you be my friend.

Annie (age 11) said, "I make friends fast. I make friends real quick. But when it's time to leave I start crying."

Theme G: I Try To Follow The Rules So That We Don't Get Thrown Out Of Here On My Account.

Many of the children were acutely aware of the rules and regulations in the current shelter. For example, Christina (age 11) said, "They don't want no fights or nothing. They could throw you out for any little thing." For example, Jennifer (age 13) was also aware of a rule against fighting in the shelter. She said, "I see the kids downstairs start with other kids then I figure they'll start with me. Then I might have to fight and get my mother put out. So that's why I stay upstairs out of trouble.

Annie was also aware of rules at the hotel. and fearful of being asked to leave. She said,

> I didn't like to go outside. If the security guards
> catch us in the hallway, they be real mad and
> probably put a stop. And then we could get thrown
> out. If my mother got to go outside and we run
> around in the hallway, then my mother can get
> throwed out.

Theme H: My belief in God Has Helped Me Through This.

One child and two of the mothers mentioned their belief in God
as helpful. Annie (age 11) said,

> I always say, God, please let me have my
> apartment, like where we are now, just to the tip of
> the apartment, right there. Just right around the
> corner.

Isabel explained how she stopped drinking,

> I say homeless is the homeless. I keep destroying
> myself. Then I realized that's something that I
> have to take. That's something that God sent for
> me. So I had to take it. I had to accept it.

Sylvia said:

> My best decision was to walk out and see hardship.
> But I really didn't see hardship. I think that's
> because God knew I was going to make it and He
> provided a way for us to get here. Because he
> could have had a worse predicament than here.
> Because usually people don't get in here that fast.

Theme I: I Found A Job To Help My Mother With Expenses.

Only one child used this strategy but his efforts were
commendable. John (age 11) informally worked at the supermarket
putting groceries into bags and delivering them. He earned tips for
his work and said that he gave most of his money to his mother.

CATEGORY IX. VIEW OF THE FUTURE

Theme A: I Want An Apartment That We Never Have To Leave

When asked what they wanted for the future most of the mothers and children said that they wanted their own apartment. For example, Sylvia said her hope is "mainly to get my apartment so me and the kids could be comfortable." Annie (age 11) said,

> I want to get a house. I'm trying to get a house. Because it's fun to be in a house. And you feel safe and you don't have to be around people so much.

Dana (age 12) said she was looking forward to not having to pack and unpack every six months.

Theme B: After We Move I Hope Our Problems Will Disappear.

Two of the mothers expressed the hope that their problems would clear up once they moved to their own apartment. For example, Isabel expressed the hope that her son, Jose (age 13) would behave better at home and school after they moved. Similarly, Sylvia was hopeful that her son Jason (age 5) would stop fighting in school once she moved and transferred him to a school near her new apartment.

Theme C: I Want To Work So I Can Get Off Welfare.

Five of the six mothers expressed the desire to find a job so they could earn more money than welfare provides. The sixth mother, Linda, does not want to work while her children are young because she wants to be home to care for them. However, she would like to work when her children are older. Three of the mothers were involved in job training programs. Maria said,

> I want to get off this welfare. It don't even help really. I got three kids. So I don't buy one a pair of sneakers and not the other one. So when I buy I stay broke.

Subtheme 1 : When I grow up I want to get a good job. Almost all the children knew what kind of jobs they wanted when they grow up.

For example, Dana (age 12) said, "In the future, I hope I become a lawyer so that way I will be able to support my mother and sister." Alison (age 8) said "when I grow up I want to be a doctor, a singer and a dancer." Jimmy (age 11) said that he wants to be a fireman when he grows up.

Theme D: I'd Like To Live In A World Without Homelessness.

This theme was mentioned by one child but seemed particularly meaningful. Christina (age 11) said,

> I would like to see people helping each other. I wouldn't let anybody be homeless. There would be no homes in the street. There won't be no killing and there won't be no drugs.

VI

Discussion, Recommendations and Summary

INTRODUCTION

This study explored the impact of homelessness on a small group of mothers and their school age children who lived in one temporary shelter in an urban setting. The study described how these families became homeless, how they perceived the shelter system past and present, their emotional responses to their experience, the impact of homelessness on their relationships, academic consequences for children, their supports and coping strategies and their view of the future. In this chapter these findings will be discussed followed by practical implications and suggestions for future research.

DISCUSSION OF FINDINGS

Reasons for Homelessness

All six families were homeless because they were unable to find an apartment they could afford with the amount of money allocated for rent by the welfare system. The amount allocated is much less than the average rent in New York City. For example, in 1988 welfare provided a family of four $312 for rent (Citizen's Committee for Children of New York, 1988). But, the vacancy rate for apartments renting for less than $300 per month had fallen to under one per cent (Citizen's Committee for Children of New York, 1988). Families are, thus, in an impossible situation unless they obtain subsidized city housing. In addition, some reasons the families in this study gave for leaving their last place of residence included: eviction, an abusive husband, a dangerous living situation, or an apartment where they were living with relatives. These reasons for homelessness are similar to those found in other studies of homeless families (Citizen's Committee for Children of New York, 1988; Simpson & Kilduff, 1984; Seltser & Miller, 1992). All six families spent some time living with relatives before they entered the shelter system. Mothers and children recalled overcrowded conditions as well as conflicts with their hosts. In their interviews they conveyed feelings of being unwelcome and unwanted in these households. This pattern of living with another family before entering the shelter system is common (Citizen's Committee for Children of New York, 1988). The number of families living doubled up with relatives in the public housing projects in New York City is estimated to be as high as 100,000 (Citizen's Committee for Children of New York, 1988). Therefore, many low income families are at risk of becoming homeless when these arrangements fail. All the families in this study found such living arrangements unbearable after varying amounts of time and were either asked to leave or left by choice. The Stanford Center for Families, Children and Youth (1991) in their study which compared homeless families with families at risk for homelessness found that while both groups stayed with relatives in order to avoid homelessness, living conditions were much more overcrowded for the families who became homeless. The same study found that families with low levels of social support were more likely to become homeless because they had fewer and less reliable relatives to stay with when they lost their housing.

Experiences in the Shelter System: Past and Present

All the families experienced homelessness as a crisis. However, families differed in their exposure to the stress and danger associated with homelessness in the time they spent in the system and the places to which they were sent. Families were sent to large barracks shelters or to hotels before arriving at the current shelter, which is called a Tier II transitional housing facility. Five families spent some time in the barracks shelters and five families spent time in the hotels before being placed in the current shelter. In general, the families conveyed the feeling that they were miserable in most of the shelters and hotels they were placed in before the current placement. In the hotels, mothers and children reported a pervasive sense of danger that led to fear and stress. Mothers and children reportedly witnessed fires, fights, drug dealing and stealing in the hotels. Some participants also said that they heard about people getting shot and killed in the hotels. This fear of danger often led mothers to stay in their hotel room and to restrict their children to the room to protect them. Mothers and children reported feeling isolated as it was difficult to meet other people while inside the room. This confirms the findings of the Community Service Society of New York (1984) which found considerable violence and criminal activity in the hotels. In addition, families felt they were dehumanized and mistreated by people whom they thought were supposed to help them. Several mothers said that they were sent by city workers aimlessly from shelter to shelter when they first entered the system. Many families reported that they arrived at a shelter or hotel and had to return to the welfare center because there were no vacancies. At the shelters, the rules and regulations often seemed punitive and the workers seemed uncaring.

Families also reported that essential tasks such as sleeping and eating were stressful. In the shelters, meals were served at a specific time in a cafeteria and no choice was available. Children in particular strongly disliked the food and some even felt it made them sick. In the hotels, families were expected to provide their own meals but kitchen facilities were not available. They were given more money and fewer food stamps and told to eat in restaurants. However, this suggestion was not practical due to the high cost of eating out. Most mothers managed to set up makeshift kitchens in their room with hot plates and small refrigerators. However, mothers found it difficult to prepare meals with these appliances and risked being caught for breaking hotel rules.

Sleeping arrangements in the shelters and hotels were also far from ideal. In the hotels, family members were sometimes required to share beds. The rooms were small and overcrowded. In the barracks shelters, families slept in a large room with many other families. Some mothers and children had difficulty sleeping in both types of shelter due to the lack or privacy or the sense of danger mentioned earlier. A study conducted by the Citizen's Committee for the Children of New York (1988) found that children were often unable to sleep in barracks shelters.

Although the mothers and children reported mostly negative and stressful events at the hotels and shelters, some participants had positive feelings about some of the places they stayed. One mother and children in two families said they liked one of the hotels they stayed in. The children felt safe and had friends to play with. The mother felt the staff was caring and helpful. The hotels they liked were small and located in residential areas in contrast to the hotels described above which were large and located in urban centers. Some children also felt positively about the barracks shelters because of the opportunities for socialization. They were able to make friends easily because everyone was in such proximity to each other.

A review of the positive and negative qualities these families reported while in the shelter system leads to suggestions of what they hoped to find in an ideal shelter. It seems likely that such a shelter would be safe, provide adequate facilities such as a enough beds and a kitchen, provide private space for each family, be small in size, located in a residential neighborhood, provide caring and helpful staff and provide opportunities for social interaction. Many families thought they had found such a perfect shelter when they arrived at their current placement.

All families were much happier with the current shelter because of its safe, homelike atmosphere and support services. Mothers and children felt protected by the shelter staff who they thought would evict anyone who endangered other residents. The families were also very pleased with the private apartments that included bedrooms, kitchens and bathrooms. In addition, it seems likely that in this shelter the families received more support than ever before in their lives. Many mothers took advantage of opportunities to improve their skills through educational and job training programs. They also seemed to benefit from the support and educational groups run by the shelter that helped them to cope with emotional reactions to homelessness as well as improve parenting and other coping and self-help skills.

Still, mothers and children were aware that this was not their permanent home and many wished that it was. There seemed to be a decrease in anxiety and increased sense of stability since mothers and some children knew that this was the last placement before they moved into their own apartment. Still, many participants worried about when and where they would be moving.

Emotional Consequences

Based on observation and interview report many participants seemed to experience depression and anxiety related to homelessness. This finding is similar to research that found that anxiety and severe depression were common in children living in a Boston shelter (Bassuk & Rubin, 1987). Zina, Wells and Freedman (1994) found in their study of sheltered homeless children in Los Angeles that the majority (78 percent) suffered from depression, behavioral problems or severe academic problems. Another study of homeless children eight to twelve years old (Wagner & Menke, 1991) found that dysphoria and depression were frequently present in their sample and more than forty percent required a psychiatric referral.. Rog, McCombs-Thornton, Gilbert-Mongelli, Brito and Halupka (1995) also found that homeless mothers in their study exhibited high levels of depression. In the current study, mothers reported that they experienced feelings of anxiety because they did not know what would happen to their family once they entered the shelter system. Children also experienced anxiety related to the uncertainty of their situation. Uncertainty and ambiguity can make events more stressful (Lazarus & Folkman, 1984). Mothers and children also expressed anxiety due to a fear of danger in the shelters. Mothers stated that they felt depressed about their situation and cried frequently especially when they first entered the system. One mother expressed feeling so depressed and hopeless when first placed in a welfare hotel that she said she experienced suicidal thoughts and drank alcohol frequently.

Some mothers thought that homelessness reflected negatively on themselves. Two mothers mentioned feeling guilty and questioning whether they were a good mother for allowing this to happen to their family. Feelings of negative self worth such as these may have led to feelings of depression in these women.

The sadness the participants experienced also seemed related to loss. All families had to cope with many losses since they became homeless. The significant losses for each person were different. Participants missed their possessions, their friends and family.

Many participants reported that they felt better and more hopeful living in the current shelter. Mothers reported increased self-esteem due to participation in educational and job training programs. However, based on observation, many mothers and children still looked anxious and depressed about their situation.

Participants also expressed anger in response to their situation. Two mothers seemed angry that they had become homeless due to eviction by landlords. Children reported they were taunted by peers about living in the shelter, which made them angry. Mothers also reported feeling angry when their children were teased and stigmatized because they are homeless. Based on observation some children also were dressed in torn clothing, which may have added to their difficulties with others. It is easy to speculate upon the negative effect this taunting may have had on the children's self-concept and self-esteem. It seemed that angry feelings were reflected in some children's behavioral difficulties such as fighting. Redmond and Brackman (1990) found angry, acting out behavior to be common in children who lived in shelters.

Several mothers and children also reported health problems such as headaches and asthma that were exacerbated by the stress of the homeless situation. Stress related to fear, anger and anxiety and certain types of illness are thought to be related (Lazarus & Folkman, 1984).

Academic Consequences

The academic consequences of homelessness for children were profound. Many children reported that they missed school frequently when they moved and almost all were forced to switch schools one or more times following multiple moves. Homeless children frequently miss school when their parents move to a shelter (Advocates for Children, 1989). This situation used to be more common before Congress passed the McKinney Act which states that homeless children must be allowed to remain at the school near their former place of residence or be allowed to register at the school near the shelter. Before the act, parents were often unable to register their children at school because they did not have a permanent place of residence. Unfortunately, returning to the former school requires long trips as families are often placed great distances from their former neighborhoods.

Switching schools caused children considerable anxiety and distress. Children who were forced to do so in the middle of the school year missed much material and had a hard time keeping up with the work. Some children had to repeat a grade in school because they were unable to catch up when placed in a new school. They also arrived in school tired because of disrupted sleep. In addition, the children who arrived in New York from Puerto Rico had difficulty because of the switch from Spanish to English in school. For example, one child who had been in a program for gifted children in Puerto Rico was given a reading test in English when she entered school here. She said that she failed the test because she was not accustomed to reading in English and was held back a grade.

In addition, children enjoyed school for its social aspects. Some children seemed to care less about moving to another shelter than about a switch of schools. School for children was an important place of refuge from the stress of the shelters. Similarly, Horowitz, Springer and Kose (1988) found that the school environment facilitated hotel children's adaptation to their stressful environment.

Children made friends in school and did not want to lose them. One of the more stressful aspects of switching schools for the children seemed to be the need to make new friends. Several children mentioned how difficult meeting new friends was for them. Many children spent much of their time in school because they attended an after school program four days during the week until six o'clock at night.

According to Erikson (1963) in our society school is critical for children to learn the tasks necessary to be productive adults. Children will develop a sense of "industry" or "inferiority" dependent on how they feel they perform relative to other children. Children such as the homeless who find it difficult or impossible to keep up with their peers in school will most likely develop a sense of inferiority that can have lasting effects throughout their lives.

The school histories of the fourteen children in this study varied. Six children were at the correct grade for their age. Two children were one grade below and three were two grades below where they should have been in school. Two children were in special education classes due to their behavior. Another child was in a special class for learning problems. All the children in special education had been placed there before their family became homeless. The number of times each child switched school since their family left their former apartment ranged from one to four.

Surprisingly, some children were able to remain on grade level and were said to be doing well in school. The children who seemed to be doing better in school had switched schools less often and had mothers who valued their education and helped them negotiate the school system. For example, one mother took her children to school and was told they should be placed in a lower grade. She refused to allow this and produced their report cards. Another mother with two children on grade level said that she repeatedly tells her children how sorry she is that she dropped out of school and how much harder it is to get her high school equivalency now.

In addition, how children understand and cope with homelessness may impact on their academic success. One study of two hundred homeless children ages six to twelve years old (Timberlake, 1994) found differences in psychosocial functioning in school as well as in children's understanding of and coping with homelessness between subjects who were doing well academically and those who had academic problems.

Homeless children are probably at great risk for dropping out of school due to all the difficulties they encounter there. This problem is not limited to homeless children as many children in New York State drop out of before graduating from high school. According to the New York State Education department (1986) this rate is particularly high for black and Hispanic youth and is estimated at 54 percent for black students and 60 percent for Hispanic students. However homelessness may add to this already prevalent problem for poor, minority children who find it difficult to stay in school for many other reasons.

Relationships and Supports

Much research has pointed to the moderating effect of social support on stress for people (Eckenrode & Gore, 1981). The women and children in this study all used some forms of social support. They stated that they received support from immediate family members, the mother's or father's family of origin, friends and organizations in the community. They used these sources of support to varying degrees.

Five women in the study were involved with a man who might or might not be the father of one or more of her children. They said that the men helped them emotionally and financially. But, men were described as unreliable and the women were reluctant to depend on them. The current shelter was one of the few that seemed to promote relationships between men and women. The mothers reported that many of the other hotels and shelters did not allow visitors This made it difficult to maintain their relationships with men, which were an important source of support. In the current shelter many men seemed to stay with the women for several days at a time and in two cases even seemed to be living with them. This was not possible in the other places. The lack of financial support from the men was generally due to inconsistent work or unemployment. This is understandable as unemployment rates for minority men are very high (Moore Hines & Boyd-Franklin, 1982).

Most children seemed close to their mothers and to rely on them for help. Their mothers have been the only consistent adult in their lives both before and during the homeless experience. Mothers who had older daughters tended to have a very close relationship with them. Mothers relied on their older children to help with and watch the younger children at times. The older children did not seem to mind. Serving in a parental role can be a positive experience for children and help to buffer them from the impact of stress (Werner & Smith, 1982). Children also relied heavily on their friends for support. Many older children had one or two close friends who were very important to them.

Five of the six families still relied on the support and help of their family of origin. Unfortunately families were often placed far from their old neighborhoods and the relationships they still had there. All families in the current shelter were far from their old neighborhood. Many still traveled back to visit relatives on the weekends or during the summer. However, they were unable to rely on their family for help on a daily basis because they were often too far away. This may have been particularly stressful for the families in this study as black and Hispanic families tend to rely heavily on their family for help (Badillo-Ghali, 1977; Moore Hines & Boyd-Franklin, 1982). For one family homelessness seemed to strain her relationships with family members who did not provide as much support as she would have liked.

Literature on resilient children has found that children who are better able to cope with their situation often develop relationships with other adults outside the family such as grandparents, teachers or clergy members (Werner, 1988; Garmezy, 1987; Fisher et al., 1987; Rutter, 1987; Anthony, 1974). Unfortunately homeless children have little opportunity to form such relationships or to continue them due to separation from their community of origin and frequent subsequent moves.

Most of the mothers developed friendships with at least one other woman in the shelter who provided social companionship as well as information about negotiating the system. Some mothers seemed part of an informal support network in which women helped each other when necessary with childcare or loans of money. However, some women were wary about involvement with the other residents who could make life very difficult if they so chose. For example, one mother found that when she did not want to lend other residents food or money they falsely reported her to the authorities for child abuse that led to an investigation. This social network may be similar to the one observed by Stack (1974) in her study of low income women with positive and negative benefits for participants. However, expectations and roles may be different due to the transient nature of relationships. It might be easier for some women to ask for favors and not return them since they probably will move away soon.

All mothers took part in some support services available at the shelter. However, only two of the mothers used organizations within the community for support. This points to the importance of having services available and easily accessible in shelters. It is likely that fewer mothers would have participated in support groups, counseling, job training or educational programs if they were not offered at the shelter.

Coping Strategies

Mothers and children in this study used several coping strategies. Mothers learned to become their own advocates and to work around and use the system to meet their needs. For example, several mothers thought they had successfully obtained a better placement within the shelter system for their families. Women reported that they turned down placements that they did not want and asked for placements they preferred. Two women viewed entering the shelter system as a strategy to get their own apartment in city-owned housing. They were aware that families who were homeless received priority placement. Both mothers said that they had been on waiting lists for years. According to Lazarus and Folkman (1984), these strategies are problem focused and used frequently when people believe it is possible to change their situation. Clearly many mothers in this study at times felt that they could improve their situation.

Unfortunately, many mothers' attempts to use problem focused strategies to improve their situation were unsuccessful. For example, two of the women attempted to take their landlord to court after they were evicted from their apartments. However, in both cases they were not successful. Dill and Feld (1982), in their study of low income mothers, found that although many of these mothers used strategies to negotiate positive change for their families their efforts were often thwarted by the bureaucratic system. These unsuccessful efforts at coping led either to depression or increased efforts at coping in these women.

The primary coping strategy used by both mothers and children was to stay by themselves and to avoid contact with other shelter residents who could cause problems. This behavior continued in the present shelter but seemed to have started in the hotels, which were more dangerous. Mothers encouraged their children, especially girls, to stay in the apartment when they were not in school to protect them from what they perceived as a dangerous environment. Although this strategy also could be viewed as problem focused, it often seemed to have a negative effect and caused isolation for mothers and children.

Children had few opportunities to use strategies to help their families move from the shelter. One way that children seemed to feel they could contribute was through good behavior. Many children were very sensitive to the rules and regulations in effect in the places they lived. They tried to follow the rules as much as possible and were afraid that their family might be thrown out if they broke the rules. Children also used problem focused strategies to cope with losing friends each time they moved. Many of them seemed to make new friends quickly to replace the ones they lost although some found the process painful and complained of the difficulty. In Murphy and Moriarty's (1976) description of children's coping the children's attempt to follow the rules and ways of making new friends would be called active problem solving strategies.

Children and some mothers seemed to try to avoid thinking about their situation. Strategies such as these are thought to be useful in situations where people are unable to do much to change their situation (Miller, 1980). Many seemed to engage in solitary activities such as watching television and playing computer games or sleeping. Other participants became involved in more social activities. Some mothers became involved in activities at the shelter. Other children, particularly older boys, were more active and spent time outside playing sports such as football or baseball with their friends. Using Murphy and Moriarty's (1976) coping paradigm, this strategy of avoiding tension associated with an event is common in children.

Mothers also used strategies that Lazarus and Folkman (1984) have called emotion focused. These strategies are thought to be useful in situations where people have little control over the outcome of their situation. Two such strategies used by the mothers involved reminding themselves that the current shelter would be the last placement until they found their apartment and the hope that after they moved all their problems would disappear.

Two of the mothers and one child said they found comfort and help in their religious beliefs. The mothers felt that God was looking out for them and protecting them from major hardship and tragedy. One mother expressed the belief that all the trials she has had to endure were a test from God. One child stated that she prays every night for an apartment and feels that if she prays enough her prayers will be answered. Lazarus and Folkman (1984) consider religious beliefs to be an important coping resource that can increase hope as well as coping behavior.

Many women and children seemed overweight. Although this may be a subjective opinion there may be one of two reasons for this. They may be eating foods with poor nutritional value or they may be overeating as a way of coping with the stress of the situation. Two of the mothers were heavy smokers. These behaviors may have been one way these women coped with their situation. Although substance abuse did not seem to be a primary problem for the mothers in this study, several women expressed the feeling that many homeless women are drug abusers. One mother said that she drank in response to her situation. One mother admitted that she was a crack user before she became homeless but claimed she no longer used the drug. Substance abuse is an increasing problem for homeless mothers (Weinrab & Bassuk, 1990).

How people and families perceive events has been cited as critical to how they feel about them (Lazarus & Folkman, 1984; McCubbin & Patterson, 1983). Models of family coping emphasize the importance of resources and the definition the family makes of the event in determining how they cope (Hill, 1958; McCubbin & Patterson, 1983). Mothers differed in their perceptions of why they left their former place of residence. Two of the women were forced to leave by their landlords. The other four women left to improve their situation, in search of a better life for themselves and their children. These two very different circumstances seemed to have an impact on the way the women felt about their situation and possibly how they coped with it. The women who were evicted seemed more bitter and angry and felt victimized. They blamed their landlords for their predicament. In contrast, the four women who viewed homelessness as a step toward a positive life change seemed to have a more positive attitude toward their situation. This difference seemed due to their different perceptions of the event. McCubbin and Patterson's (1983) model of family coping considers adaptation after a crisis or event. Changes that occur after the event are thought to influence future coping. This has clearly proved true for the families in this study. After they moved to the current shelter many were able to increase their coping by taking advantage of opportunities to improve their situation at the shelter.

Families differed in the resources they had available to them. For example, mothers who were involved with men may have had more money available as the men often provided some financial help even if it was inconsistent. Women involved with men may have had more emotional support and help with the children than those who were not. Families also differed in the amount of social support they had available from their extended families. These resources can have an impact on how well people are able to cope with a situation (Lazarus & Folkman, 1984).

View of the Future

Mothers and children all looked forward to moving to an apartment they would never have to leave. Mothers tended to be optimistic about the future and hoped their problems would disappear once they moved into their own apartment. For example,

two mothers hoped that their sons who had been having d
school and at home would do better once they mov
mothers also expressed the wish to continue their educati
a job so they could earn more money than what they received from
welfare benefits. All the mothers had left high school before
graduation. Most regretted this decision and were in the process of
studying for their high school equivalency exam. One mother had
already obtained this degree. No child expressed the desire to be on
welfare when they grew up and many had specific careers in mind.

Unfortunately, when most of these women move into
apartments their access to support services, educational and job
training programs such as those provided at the shelter will be much
more difficult. I hope they will be able to follow through on their
plans to improve their situation. Staff at the shelter do follow up
with the families once they move and families are welcome to
continue to participate in the activities at the shelter.

Most of the children looked forward to moving with a
combination of hope and anxiety. They very much wanted their
own apartment because of the security but did not want to leave
their current school and friends. Three children were hopeful that
they would not have to leave their current school and neighborhood
because they were going to obtain an apartment near the shelter.

Other Concerns

When studying the impact of homelessness on these families, it
is important to consider other variables in the lives of the families
that may provide additional stress. Factors such as poverty,
violence, single parent status and limited education all added to the
difficulties faced by these families. It is difficult to parcel out what
is due to homelessness per se and what is due to other factors. For
example, many of these families live with drugs and violence in
their neighborhood even when they are not homeless and living in
the projects. Almost all the families have struggled with financial
hardship on a continuing basis. Bassuk (1986) found that it is the
combined effects of poverty, violence and deprivation that impact
on homeless mothers and children. Homeless children are
vulnerable to many risks common to children of poverty such as
poor prenatal care, low birthweight, infant mortality and social and
psychological stress that exacerbate health problems (Vermund,
Belmar & Drucker, 1987). In fact, poverty may place homeless
children at risk for many problems before and after they are
homeless. For example, one study (Ziesemer, Marcoux & Marwell,
1994) which compared academic performance, adaptive functioning

and problem behaviors of elementary school age children who were homeless with those of low socioeconomic status who had experienced frequent moves found no difference between the two groups. However, both groups demonstrated significantly more problems than the general population. Another study (Masten, Miliotis, Graham-Bermann, Ramirez & Neeman, 1993) which compared homeless children with a group of low income children found some differences between the two groups. They found behavioral problems were higher for homeless children particularly in antisocial behavior. However, the researchers found that behavior problems in both groups were more related to other factors commonly associated with poverty and suggest that the two groups share many of the same risks to emotional adjustment.

Many mothers in this study also have experienced multiple losses in their lives. Two of them lost their mothers at a very early age, others have lost husbands and lovers to drugs and jail and some have lost contact with their families who still reside in Puerto Rico. These factors can take their toll emotionally on the families and reduce their ability to cope with their situation.

REFLECTIONS OF THE INVESTIGATOR

Although I live in the same city as the homeless families do, my experience is very different. As an adult I have been able to earn enough money to share the expenses with my husband. Even if one of us lost our jobs we could fall back on our parents to help and tide us over until we found a new job. I grew up in a middle class family in a large apartment. I took many things for granted such as the ability of my parents to provide for me financially and experienced a sense of security and stability these children lack. As I interviewed the families for this study, I was struck by the adversity these mothers and children faced and how they tried to cope with it.

When I set out to do this research I hoped to find some children who were not negatively touched by the homeless experience, the so-called invulnerables. But, as I interviewed the children and mothers, I found that the experience affected negatively on all. Some children seemed to be doing better than others, but most children seemed anxious or depressed. The poverty in some families was striking and disturbing. It was difficult to see children wearing torn clothing and having few if any toys to play with and to hear them worry about safety and crime.

Among the mothers I interviewed I expected to see more disturbed individuals. Many of the women exhibited strengths in coping with their situation. This is consistent with the findings of a recent qualitative study which found many self-reported strengths in the homeless mothers interviewed (Banyard & Graham-Bermann, 1995). In fact, the homeless women in my study seemed very similar to their counterparts living in city housing projects. The difference was that they were not protected from eviction and rent raises as people in the housing projects are. These are women who cannot find a place to live because there are few apartments other than projects that they can afford.

METHODOLOGICAL CONSIDERATIONS

An in-depth interview was used to attempt to understand the experience of mothers and children who had been homeless. Through these interviews it was possible to obtain considerable information on each participant's perceptions and coping strategies as they related to the homeless experience. The open ended nature of the interviews allowed participants to bring up material that was not anticipated. Usually, two interviews were conducted with each participant. The option of a second interview gave me the opportunity to return after having listened to the first interview and clarify any points that were not clear and to ask further questions if necessary.

Data collection and analysis were stressful. Initially I felt uncomfortable conducting the interviews in the apartments for safety reasons. I expected a shelter to be a dangerous place. However, the more time I spent there the more comfortable I felt. Just as the participants reported, the shelter felt safe. After the first interviews I realized the benefits of interviewing the families in their apartments. Observations of family life were plentiful. In addition, conducting the interviews in the family's apartment seemed to help them feel comfortable. But, this at times made it difficult to find a quiet spot to conduct the interview. The apartments were not very large and sometimes the only place to conduct the interview was a corner of the living room. Mothers with young children needed to watch them while the interview was conducted.

Initially I worried about finding enough interested families to participate in the study. However, this fear was unfounded as many more families were interested then I was able to use. I soon found it was difficult to schedule appointments with the families as all except one did not have phones. Sometimes it took several visits before I found them at home and could schedule an appointment. Even when the appointments were scheduled sometimes the family would not be home at the appointed time. It took persistence in order schedule and follow-up on all the interviews.

After the interviews were transcribed I was left with many pages of data for analysis. It was a formidable task to go through all this data and organize the interview material around topics that seemed meaningful for most of the participants. The word processing program on my computer was invaluable for this process. In addition, profiles were created using as much verbatim material as possible so that the picture of the individual families would not be lost. However, it sometimes seemed that I included too many families in the study to cover adequately as there was so much information to sort through.

Throughout the project I worked closely with another researcher, which was invaluable. It was helpful to share observations and concerns about the project on an ongoing basis. During the data analysis phase we went over interviews together and discussed the emerging coding categories. This process was important and helpful in refining and developing the themes and categories.

SUGGESTIONS FOR FUTURE RESEARCH

Future research is important to investigate how other homeless families perceive their experience. The families in this study are not necessarily representative of the population of homeless families. The families volunteered for this study. For example, some mothers referred to other homeless women who were using drugs. However, none of the participants seemed to be drug abusers and such people might be less likely to volunteer for a study.

The same type of study might provide different results with different participants. Single mothers are not the only type of homeless family. There are intact families as well as single fathers. The experience might be different for those families.

This study leaves unanswered questions about how the families will fare once they leave the shelter. Will they be able to make it on their own? Will they become homeless again? Will they continue job training or educational programs that they began at the shelter? How will the children fare? Will they be less anxious or depressed once they have their own apartment? An interesting study would be to follow families who have been homeless to try to provide some answers to these and other questions. In addition, a study of people who moved into permanent housing and succeeded in improving their lives would be valuable. Some recent studies have begun to try to answer similar questions (Shlay, 1994; Helvie & Alexies, 1992; Weitzman & Berry, 1994).

Children in this study reported difficulties in school. It would be of great interest to go to schools and observe homeless children there. A study of homeless children in school would provide additional information about how they function and cope in academic situations. Children could be observed in the school setting and interviewed about their experience. Teachers and other professionals could also be interviewed to obtain information on their observations and interactions with homeless children. It would also be interesting to interview the homeless children who seem to be doing well academically. Such a study would possibly provide a greater understanding of resiliency and coping in homeless children.

This study also raises questions about how different the homeless families actually are from low income families in city housing. It would be of interest to compare families living in the shelter with families from similar socioeconomic and cultural backgrounds who are living in the public housing projects to try to differentiate what if anything separates these two groups. Recent studies have started to make comparisons between these two groups (Ziesemer, Marcoux & Marwell, 1994; Masten, Miliotis, Graham-Bermann, Ramirez & Neeman, 1993; Stanford Center for the Study of Families, Children and Youth, 1991).

Children in this study were within a limited age range (5-13). Even within the selected age range, children of different ages seemed to respond differently to the homeless experience. It would be valuable to document developmental differences more closely. For example, the two oldest participants in this study were ages 12 and 13, they seemed to have the most negative attitude toward school. It would be interesting to study the impact of homelessness on adolescents. The results might be very different. Another age group that was not in this study was preschoolers. Although some mothers had children of this age it was not possible to interview them due to the linguistic requirements of such a task. Based on observation and parental report these children seemed to have problems related to homelessness.

RECOMMENDATIONS

Homelessness has increased, particularly in low income families. This study was small but if these results are representative of the larger group, then these recommendations would hold. The problem of homeless families is a complex one and will not begin to be solved until society makes many changes in the current system of providing for low income families who are placed in an impossible situation. They are asked to find housing that is nonexistent at the price they are unable to pay. Unless the welfare housing allowance increases or the government builds more low income housing, people will frequently be faced with homelessness. Many people do not have the skills necessary to find jobs or jobs are not available. Solutions to the problem of homeless families in New York include building more low cost housing. In addition, another important factor is to make sure that children stay in school and learn skills that will help them find employment once they graduate. Mothers should be encouraged to supplement the allowance they receive from welfare for housing by working part time.

It is clear that in an attempt to provide emergency shelter for homeless families as quickly as possible, the emotional needs of the children are being neglected. Based on what the children in this study have reported the number of moves and school changes as well as loss of contact with friends and relatives and loss of belongings all contribute to the stress experienced when their families become homeless. In addition, placement in dangerous environments add to their distress. If the number of moves and school changes could be minimized by placing families once rather than many times, in a safe environment such as the transitional shelter described in this study, it would do a lot to alleviate the stress the children experience and would help decrease emotional and academic consequences.

It might be possible to decrease the number of moves for some families if becoming homeless was not almost necessary for those who hope to find subsidized housing. While many families do not have relatives they can stay with for an extended period of time, some families do have such an option available. Some of the families mentioned that they were unable to get the help they needed in finding an apartment they could afford if they continued to live with relatives. If families living doubled up with relatives were viewed as at risk for homelessness and given more assistance in finding housing, the urgency for immediate shelter placement might be averted. In addition, families living in such crowded conditions with relatives often face many conflicts in getting along with their hosts. If early intervention services such as family therapy and crisis counseling could be provided, some families might be able to stay with their hosts until an appropriate transitional shelter or apartment became available.

Based on the findings of this study and others (DiBlasio & Belcher, 1992, 1995), transitional shelters appear to provide families with the living conditions and services they need while they locate permanent housing. The families seemed to experience significantly less stress in the transitional shelter than in the other shelters or hotels they had stayed in before such placement. This study also suggests that homeless families benefit from support services provided in the transitional shelter such as job training, preparation for High School equivalency exams, child care, support groups and counseling. If additional transitional shelters were available and families were immediately placed in such a setting, it seems likely that they would fare better. Yet, recently researchers have begun to question the need for transitional shelters and instead suggest that families be placed in permanent housing with support services available (Rog, Holupka & McCombs-Thornton, 1995; Weinreb & Buckner, 1993; Friedmutter, 1989). This new model has been called services-enriched housing. Further research is necessary to help determine if this solution best meets the needs of homeless families.

Caseworkers and other professionals who work with homeless families should be alert for symptoms of anxiety and depression in the mothers and children. in their caseload. Based on the literature that suggests a high frequency of emotional disorders in this population (Bassuk & Rubin, 1987; Zina, Wells & Freedman, 1994; Wagner & Menke, 1991), it would be worthwhile when possible to screen all family members who enter a shelter for symptoms that might require intervention. All mothers and children who are experiencing significant levels of anxiety, depression or other emotional problems should be referred for treatment as soon as possible.

Schools can and should help homeless children cope with their situation. Professionals, such as school psychologists and teachers, who work with homeless children in schools are in an excellent position to help the children cope with their feelings regarding their experience. Teachers can increase their sensitivity to the stress experienced by these children and develop strategies to help homeless children cope more successfully in the classroom. For example, Long and Duffner (1980) suggest many such strategies for teachers to use to increase coping in distressed children such as forming a helping adult relationship, lowering school pressure, redirecting feelings into acceptable behavior, accepting disappointment and failure, reducing stress by helping less fortunate students, separating from the setting and helping the student seek professional help. Gewirtzman and Fodor (1987) discussed the psychological impact of rootlessness on children living in welfare hotels and recommended providing a nonthreatening classroom environment and helping the children express their fears and frustrations. Daniels (1992) presents an intervention program for counselors in the elementary school setting designed to help promote personal and educational growth of homeless children.

Activities that help promote self-esteem are important. All staff need to be aware of the background of these children and to be available to provide them with the help and support they need. Crisis intervention and support groups could help these children cope with their situation and the school environment. In addition, such professionals need to be observant and sensitive to the needs of these children and make appropriate referrals for tutoring and counseling as necessary. Much work also needs to be done with all children as the children in this study reported tension and conflict between themselves and housed classmates. Discussion groups might be helpful in decreasing tension and promoting positive interactions between all children.

SUMMARY

This study explored and described the experience of homelessness for low income, single parent families consisting of mothers and children living in one temporary urban shelter. Stress and coping theory were described to provide a theoretical framework for the study. Literature on homeless families, poverty, sociocultural factors, stress associated with losing one's home and finding shelter, homelessness as trauma, coping strategies and social supports were presented and contributed to the understanding of the experience of homeless families.

Six families residing in one transitional shelter participated in the study. A total of six mothers and fourteen children, ages five to thirteen, were interviewed. The amount of time families spent in the shelter system before placement in the current shelter ranged from four and one half months to three years. The number of children in each family ranged from two to five. All families were headed by a single mother. Three families were Black and three were Hispanic. Semi-structured, in-depth interviews were conducted. The interviews were open ended and enabled the women and children to introduce unanticipated topics. The interviews were tape recorded and transcribed. They were then analyzed and organized into themes and categories. In the write-up, all identifying features were changed to maintain confidentiality. Profiles of the participants in the study were distilled from the analysis based on a combination of narrative and direct quotes. The categories described major areas of importance for the whole group. The categories were: reasons for becoming homeless, experiences in the shelter system past and present, emotional consequences, academic consequences, impact on relationships, supports, coping strategies and view of the future.

In summary, these families found most hotels and shelters to be dangerous, dehumanizing, isolating and stressful places. However, contrary to popular belief, participants found some smaller hotels to be safe and adequate for their temporary needs. Some children also liked the congregate shelters where they were able to make friends easily. All families preferred the current shelter in which they lived in private apartment-style units with kitchens and baths. In contrast to how the families felt in many hotels and shelters, they felt safe in their current placement. The shelter provided many support services such as counseling, support groups, educational and job training programs. All mothers participated in these activities to some degree and seemed to feel good about making positive changes in their lives. Children participated in recreational programs and summer day camp. Based on observation and report many mothers and children seemed anxious or depressed. One source of anxiety seemed to be uncertainty about their situation. Depression seemed related to feelings of hopelessness and loss. Academic consequences were particularly profound for children. Switching schools frequently caused considerable anxiety and distress. Factors such as poverty, single parent status, low educational background all added to the difficulties faced by these families. All women and children used some forms of social support. Mothers reported that they received emotional and financial support from men with whom they were in a relationship. They also received support from their children and extended family members. Children relied on their mothers and friends for support. Coping strategies included learning to use the system to their advantage (mothers), avoiding problems by staying alone or with family (mothers and children), drinking alcohol (mothers), keeping busy so that they don't think about their situation too much (mothers and children), learning and following the rules of the shelter (children) and believing in God (mothers and children). In the future, mothers and children all expressed the desire to have their own apartment that they will never have to leave. Most of the mothers expressed the desire to work and get off welfare.

Bibliography

Agar, M. (1980). *The professional stranger: An informal introduction to ethnography.* New York: Academic Press.

American Psychiatric Association (1987). *Diagnostic and statistical manual of mental disorders, revised.* Washington, DC: American Psychiatric Association.

Anthony, E. J. (1987). Children at high risk for psychosis growing up successfully. In E. J. Anthony & B. Cohler (Eds.), *The invulnerable child* (pp.147-184). New York: Guilford Press.

_____. (1974). The syndrome of the psychologically invulnerable child. In E. J. Anthony & C. Koupernik (Eds.), *The child in his family: Children at psychiatric risk* (International Yearbook, Vol. 3). New York: Wiley.

Badillo-Ghalli, S. (1974). Culture sensitivity and the Puerto Rican client. *Social Casework, 55*(1), 100-110.

Banyard, V.L. & Graham-Bermann, S.A. (1995). Building an empowerment policy paradigm: Self-reported strengths of homeless mothers. *American Journal of Orthopsychiatry,* 65,479-491.

Bassuk, E. (1993). Homeless women: Economic and social issues. *American Journal of Orthopsychiatry, 63,* 341-347.

_____. (1990). Who are the homeless families? Characteristics of sheltered mothers and children. *Community Mental Health Journal, 26,* 425-434.

_____. (1987). The feminization of homelessness: Families in Boston shelters. *American Journal of Social Psychiatry,* 7(1), 19-23.

_____. (1986). Homeless families: Single mothers and their children in Boston shelters. *New Directions for Mental Health Services, 30,* 45-53.

Bassuk, E. & Rosenberg, L. (1988). Why does family homelessness occur? A case control study. *American Journal of Public Health, 78,* 783-788.

Bassuk, E. & Rubin, L. (1987). Homeless children: A neglected population. *American Journal of Orthopsychiatry, 57*(2), 279-286.

Belle, D. (1982). Social ties and social support. In D. Belle, (Ed.), *Lives in stress.* Beverly Hills, CA: Sage.

Belle, D. & Dill, D. (1982). Research methods and sample characteristics. In D. Belle, (Ed.), *Lives in stress.* Beverly Hills, CA: Sage.

Bleuler, M. (1984). Different forms of childhood stress and patterns of adult psychiatric outcome. In N. F. Watt, E. J. Anthony, L. C. Wynne & J. Rolf (Eds.), *Children at risk for schizophrenia: A longitudinal perspective.* Cambridge, England: Cambridge University Press.

Bogdan, R. & Bicklen, S. (1982). *Qualitative research for education.* Boston: Allyn and Bacon.

Brown, S. & Harris, T. (1978). *The social origins of depression.* New York: Free Press.

Browne, A. (1993). Family violence and homelessness: The relevance of trauma histories in the lives of homeless women. *American Journal of Orthopsychiatry,* 63, 370-383.

Bussis, A., Chittenden, E. & Amarel, M. (1976). *Beyond Surface Curriculum.* Boulder, CO: Westview Press.

Citizen's Committee for Children of New York (1988). *Children in storage: families in New York City's barracks-style shelters.* New York: Citizen's Committee for Children of New York.

_____. (1984). *7000 homeless children: the crisis continues.* New York: Citizen's Committee for Children of New York.

Coalition for the Homeless. (1984). *Perchance to sleep: homeless children without shelter in New York City.* New York: Coalition for the Homeless.

Cobb, S. (1976). Social support as a moderator of life stress. *Psychosomatic Medicine.* 38, 306-314.

Committee on Government Operations, (1986). *Homeless families: A neglected crisis.* Washington, DC: U.S. Government Printing Office.

Dail, P. (1990). The psychosocial context of homeless mothers with young children: program and policy implications. *Child Welfare,* LXIX (4).

Daniels, J. (1992). Empowering homeless children through school counseling. *Elementary School Guidance and Counseling,* 27 (2), 104-112.

D'Ercole, A. & Struening, E. (1990). Victimization among homeless women: Implications for service delivery. *Journal of Community Psychology,* 18, 141-152.

DiBlasio, F. & Belcher, J. (1995). Gender differences among homeless persons: Special services for women. *American Journal of Orthopsychiatry,* 65, 131-137.

_____. (1992). Keeping homeless families together: Examining their needs. *Children and Youth Services Review,* 14, 427-438.

Dill, D. & Feld, E. (1982). The challenge of coping. In D. Belle (Ed.), *Lives in Stress* (pp. 179-196). Beverly Hills: Sage Publications.

Dohrenwend, B. (1973). Social status and stressful life events. *Journal of Personality and Social Psychiatry.* 28, 2235-235.

Dohrenwend, B. S. & Dohrenwend, B. P. (1974). *Stressful life events: Their nature and effects.* New York: John Wiley & Sons.

Eckenrode, J. & Gore, S. (1981). Stressful events and social supports: the significance of context. In B. Gottlieb (Ed.), *Social networks and social support.* Beverly Hills, CA: Sage.

Eddowes, A. & Hranitz, J. (1989). Educating children of the homeless. *Childhood Education,* 65(4), 197-200.

Egbuonu, L. & Starfiels, B. (1982). Child health and social status, *Pediatrics,* 69(5), 550-557.

Ely, M. (1984). *Beating the odds: An ethnographic interview study of young adults from the culture of poverty.* Paper presented at the Seventh Annual Conference in English Education, New York University, New York.

Ely, M., Ansul, M., Friedman, T., Garner, D. & Steinmetz, A. (1991). *Doing qualitative research: Circles within circles.* New York: Falmer Press.

Erikson, E. (1963). *Childhood and society.* New York: Norton.

_____. (1968). *Identitiy, youth and crisis.* New York: Norton.

Eth, S. & Pynoos, R. (1985). Developmental perspective on psychic trauma in childhood. In C. R. Figley (Ed.) *Trauma and it's wake.* New York: Bruner/Mazel.

Felsman, J. K. & Vaillant, G. E. (1987). Resilient children as adults: a forty year study. In E. J. Anthony & B. J. Cohler (Eds.) *The invulnerable child.* New York: Guilford Press.

Figley, C. R. (1983). Catastrophes: An overview of family reactions. In C. R. Figley & H. I. McCubbin (Eds.), *Stress and the family, Volume 2: Coping with catastrophe* (pp. 3-20). New York: Bruner Mazel.

Fisher, L., Kokes, R. F., Cole, R. E., Perkins, P. M. & Wynne, L. M. (1987). Competent children at risk: a study of well functioning offspring of disturbed parents. In E. J. Anthony & B. J. Cohler (Eds.) *The invulnerable child.* New York: Guilford Press.

Frederick, C. (1985). Children traumatized by catastrophic situations. In S. Eth & R. Pynoos (Eds.), *Post traumatic stress disorder in children* (pp.73-99). Washington, DC: American Psychiatric Press.

Friedmutter, C. (1989). *Services-enriched housing for homeless families.* Princeton, NJ: Robert Wood Johnson Foundation.

Garcia-Preto, N. (1982). Puerto Rican Families. In M. McGoldrick, J. Pearce and J. Giordano (Eds.). *Ethnicity and Family Therapy.* New York: Guilford Press.

Garmezy, N. (1987). Stress, competence and development: Continuities in the study of schizophrenic adults, children vulnerable to psychopathology, and the search for stress resistant children. *American Journal of Orthopsychiatry.* 57(2), 159-174.

_____. (1985). Stress Resistant children: The search for protective factors. In J. E. Stevenson (Ed.), *Recent research in developmental psychopathology.* Oxford: Pergamon Press.

_____. (1981). Children under stress: Perspectives on antecedents and correlates of vulnerability and resistance to psychopathology. In A. I. Rabin, J. Aronoff, A. M. Barclay, & R. Zucker (Eds.), *Further explorations in personality.* New York: Wiley-Interscience.

Garmezy, N. & Neuchterlein, K.H. (1972). Invulnerable children: The fact and fiction of competence and disadvantage. *American Journal of Orthopsychiatry,* 42, 328-329.

Gewertzman, R. & Fodor, I. (1987). The homeless child at school: From welfare hotel to classroom. *Child Welfare,* 66(3), 237-245.

Goetz, J. P. & LeCompte, M. D. (1984). *Ethnography and Qualitative Design in Educational Research.* Orlando, Fla.: Academic Press.

Goodman, L. (1991). The relationship between social support and family homelessness: A comparison of homeless housed mothers. *Journal of Community Psychology,* 19, 321-331.

Goodman, L., Saxe, L. & Harvey, M. (1991). Homelessness as psychological trauma: Broadening perspectives. *American Psychologist,* 46, 1219-1225.

Green, B.L., Wilson, J.P., & Lindy, J.D. (1985). Conceptualizing post-traumatic stress disorder: A psychosocial framework. In C.R. Figley (Ed.), *Trauma and its wake: the study and treatment of post-traumatic stress disorder.* (pp.53-69). New York: Bruner/Mazel.

Guba, E. G. & Lincoln, Y. S. (1981). *Effective Evaluation.* San Francisco: Jossey-Bass.

Helvie, C.O. & Alexy, B.B. (1992). Using after shelter case management to improve outcomes for families with children. *Public Health Reports,* 107, 585-588.

Hill, R. (1958). Sociology of marriage and family behavior, 1945 1956: A trend report and bibliography. *Current Sociology,* 7, 1098.

_____. (1949). *Families under stress: Adjustment to the crisis of war separation and reunion.* New York: Harper.

Holmes, T. H. & Masuda, M. (1974). Life change and illness susceptability. In B. S. Dohrenwend and B. P. Dohrenwend (Eds.) *Stressful life events: their nature and effects.* New York: John Wiley and Sons.

Horowitz, S., Springer, C., & Kose, G. (1988). Stress in hotel children: The effects of homelessness on attitudes towards school. *Children's Environments Quarterly,* 5(1), 34-36.

Human Resources Administration, (1986). *Characteristics and housing histories of families seeking shelter from HRA.* New York: Author.

Lazarus, R. (1966). *Psychological stress and the coping process.* New York: McGraw-Hill.

Lazarus, R. & Folkman, S. (1984). *Stress, appraisal and coping.* New York: Springer.

Lindblad-Goldberg, M., Dukes, J., & Lasley, J. Stress in black, low income, single families: Normative and dysfunctional patterns. *American Journal of Orthopsychiatry,* 58(1), 1988.

Lincoln, Y. S. & Guba, E. G. (1985). *Naturalistic Inquiry.* Beverly Hills: Sage.

Lofland, J. & Lofland, L. H. (1984). *Analyzing Social Settings.* Belmont, CA: Wadsworth.

Long, N. & Duffner, B. (1980). The stress cycle of the coping cycle? The impact of home and school stresses on pupils' classroom behavior. In N. Long, W. Morse and R. Newman (Eds.). *Conflict in the Classroom.* Belmont, CA: Wadsworth.

Makosky, V. (1982). Sources of stress: Events or conditions. In D. Belle (Ed.). *Lives in stress.* Beverly Hills, CA: Sage.

Masten, A., Miliotis, D., Graham-Bermann, S., Ramirez, M. & Neeman, J. (1993). Children in homeless families: Risks to mental health and development. *Journal of Consulting and Clinical Psychology,* 61, 335-343.

McCubbin, H. I. & Figley, C.R. (Eds.) (1983). *Stress and the family: Vols. 1-2.* New York: Bruner/Mazel.

McCubbin, H. & Patterson, J. (1983). The family stress process: The double ABCX model of adjustment and adaptation. *Marriage and Family Review,* 6, 7-37.

McLanahan, S. (1983). Family structure and stress: A longitudinal comparison of two parent and female headed families. *Journal of Marriage and Family Therapy,* 9, 347-357.

McCloyd, V.C. (1990). The impact of economic hardship on black families and children: Psychological distress, parenting and social-emotional development. *Child Development,* 61(2), 311-346.

Menaghan, E. (1983). Individual coping efforts: Moderators of the relationship between life stress and mental health outcomes. In H. Kaplan (Ed.), *Psychosocial stress: Trends in theory and research.* New York: Academic Press.

Mikhail, A. (1981). Stress: a psychophysiological conception. *Journal of Human Stress.* 7, 9-15.

Miles, M. B. & Huberman, M.A. (1984). *Qualitative data analysis: a sourcebook of new methods.* Beverly Hills, CA: Sage.

Miller, S. (1980). When is a little information a dangerous thing? Coping with stressful events by monitoring vs. blunting. In S. Levine and H. Ursin (Eds.). *Coping and health.* New York: Plenum.

Moore Hines, P. & Boyd-Franklyn, N. (1982). Black families. In M. McGoldrick, J. Pearce and J. Giordano (Eds.). *Ethnicity and Family Therapy.* New York: Guilford Press.

Morgan, T. (1991, January, 19). New York City plans to reduce beds for homeless. *New York Times.*

Murphy, L. B. (1987). Further reflections on resiliency. In E. J. Anthony & B. Cohler (Eds.), *The invulnerable child* (pp.84-105). New York: Guilford Press.

_____. (1962). *The widening world of childhood.* New York: Basic Books.

Murphy, L. B. & Moriarty, A. (1976). *Vulnerability, coping and growth: from infancy to adolescence.* New Haven, CT: Yale University Press.

New York State Council on Children and Families, (1988). *State of the child.* Albany, NY: Author.

Patton, M.Q. (1980). *Qualitative Evaluation Methods.* Newbury Park, CA: Sage.

Peters, M. & Massey, G. (1983). Mundane extreme environmental stress in family stress theories: The case of black families in white America. *Marriage and Family Review,* 6, 193-218.

Rescorla, L., Parker, R. & Stolley, P. (1991). Ability, achievement and adjustment in homeless children. *American Journal of Orthopsychiatry,* 61, 210-220.

Rodriguez, C. E., Sanchez-Korrol, V. & Alers, J. O. (1980). *The Puerto Rican Struggle: Essays on Survival.* New York: Puerto Rican Migration Research Consortium.

Rog, D.J., Holupka, S. & McCombs-Thornton, K. (1995). Implementation of the homeless families program: 1. Service models and preliminary outcomes. *American Journal of Orthopsychiatry,* 65 (4), 502-513.

Rog, D.J., McCombs-Thornton, K.L., Gilbert-Mongelli, A.M., Brito, M.C. & Holupka, C.S. (1995). Implementation of the homeless families program: 2. Characteristics , strengths, and needs of participant families. *American Journal of Orthopsychiatry,* 65 (4), 514-528.

Rossi, P.H. (1994). Troubling families: Family homelessness in America. *American Behavioral Scientist,* 37, 342-395.

Rutter, M. (1987). Psychosocial resilience and protective mechanisms. *American Journal of Orthopsychiatry.* 57 (3), 316-331.

_____. (1981). Stress, coping and development: some issues and some questions. *Journal of Child Psychiatry and Psychology.* 22, 323-356.

Seltser, B.J. & Miller, D.E. (1993). *Homeless families: The struggle for dignity.* Chicago: University of Illinois Press.

Selye, H. (1976). *The stress of life* (2nd. ed.). New York: McGraw Hill.

_____. (1974). *Stress without distress.* Philadelphia: Lippencott.

Shlay, A.B. (1994). Running on empty: Monitoring the lives and circumstances of formerly homeless families with children. *Journal of Social Distress and the Homeless,* 3 (2), 135-162.

Simpson, J. H. & Kilduff, M. (1984). *Struggling to survive in a welfare hotel.* New York: Community Service Society of New York.

Space, L. & Cromwell, R. L. (1978). Personal constructs among schizophrenic patients. In S. Schwartz (Ed.), *Language and cognition in schizophrenia.* Hillsdale, NJ: Erlbaum.

Spradley, J. (1979). *The ethnographic interview.* New York: Holt, Rinehart & Winston.

Stack, C. (1975). *All Our Kin: Strategies for Survival in a Black Community.* New York: Harper & Row.

Stanford Center for the Study of Families, Children and Youth (1991). *The Stanford studies of homeless families, children and youth.* Palo Alto, CA: Author.

Sullivan, P. & Damrosch,S. (1987). Homeless women and children. In R. D. Bingham, R. E. Green, S. B. White (Eds.), *The homeless in contemporary society.* Newbury Park, CA: Sage.

Timberlake, E.M. (1994). Children with no place to call home: Survival in the cars and on the streets. *Child and Adolescent Social Work Journal,* 11(4), 259-278.

United States Department of Housing and Urban Development (1989). *The 1988 national survey of shelters for the homeless.* Washington, DC: author.

_____. (1984). *A report to the secretary on the homeless and emergency shelters.* Washington, DC: Author.

Vermund, S. H., Belmar, R. & Drucker, E. (1987). Homelessness in New York City: The youngest victims. *New York State Journal of Medicine,* 87(1), 3-5.

Wagner, J. & Menke, E. (1991). The depression of homeless children: A focus for nursing intervention. *Issues in Comprehensive Pediatric Nursing,* 14(1), 17-29.

Wallerstein, J. & Kelly, J. (1980). *Surviving the breakup.* New York: Basic Books.

Weinreb, L. F. & Bassuk, E. L. (1990). Substance abuse: A growing problem among homeless families. *Family and Community Health,* 13(1), 55-64.

Weinreb, L.F., Browne, A. & Berson, J. (1995). Services for homeless pregnant women: Lessons from the field. *American Journal of Orthopsychiatry*, 65(4), 492-501.

Weinreb, L.F. & Buckner, J. (1993). Homeless families: Program responses and public policies. *American Journal of Orthopsychiatry*, 63, 400-409.

Weinreb, L.F. & Rossi, P. (1995). The American homeless family shelter "system." *Social Service Review*, 69, 86-107.

Weiss, R. (1968). Issues in holistic research. In H. S. Becker (Ed.), *Institutions and the person: Papers presented to Everett C. Hughs*. Chicago: Aldine.

Weitzman, B. & Berry, C. (1994). *Formerly homeless families and the transition to permanent housing: High-risk families and the role of intensive case management services*. Unpublished manuscript, New York University.

Weitzman, B., Knickman, J. & Shinn, M. (1992). Predictors of shelter use among low-income families: Psychiatric history, substance abuse and victimization. *American Journal of Public Health*, 82, 1547-1550.

Werner, E. (1989). High risk children in young adulthood: A longitudinal study from birth to thirty two years. *American Journal of Orthopsychiatry*, 59(1), 72-81.

Werner, E. & Smith, R. (1982). *Vulnerable but invincible: A study of resilient children*. New York: McGraw-Hill.

Whyte, W. F. (1984). *Learning from the field*. Beverly Hills, CA: Sage.

Wood, D.L., Valdez, R.B., Hayashi, T. & Shen. A. (1990). Homeless and housed families in Los Angeles: A study comparing demographic, economic, and family function characteristics. *American Journal of Public Health*, 80, 1049-1052.

Ziesemer, C., Marcoux, L. & Marwell, B.E. (1994). Homeless children" Are they different from other low income children? *Social Work*, 39(6), 658-668.

Zima, B.T., Wells, K.B. & Freeman, H.E. (1994). Emotional and behavioral problems and severe academic delays among sheltered homeless children in Los Angeles county. *American Journal of Public Health*, 84(2), 260-264.

Appendix A

INTERVIEW GUIDE

1. Building Rappport/Current Situation

For children: What grade are you in in school?   What do you
like/not like about school?
(probe for attitude toward school and learning, relationship to
teacher and peers)

What do you do when you're not in school?
(probe for activities after school and on weekends)

For mothers: What kinds of things are you doing now?
(probe for involvement in shelter activities, job training program,
recreational activities, parenting plus others)

2. Background Information and History

Tell me your story since you left your last apartment.
(probe for reasons for leaving, all the different places they stayed,
thoughts and feelings about each place.)

For children: Draw a picture of your last apartment and tell me
about it. This procedure will be followed for each place of shelter
they remember.

For children: Tell me about all the different schools you went to.
(probe for thoughts and feelings about moving from school to
school)

3. Perceptions of homelessness and shelter life

Why did you leave your old apartment?

For children: Draw a picture of where you live now and tell me about it.

What has been the most difficult for you since you left your apartment?

What would you tell a new person or child who just left their apartment to watch out for?

4. Coping Strategies

What has been most helpful to you during this time?

What advice would you give to a new person or child you met who just gave up their apartment?

Who has been helpful to you and your family and how have they helped?
(probe for relationships with family, friends, teachers or others)

For mothers: What plans do you have for you and your family?
(probe about how they plan to meet these)

5. Emotional and physical well-being

How do you feel about your situation?
(probe for emotional and physical information)

What were your hopes and strengths before? Now?

What did you worry about before you came to this shelter? What do you worry about now?

6. Closing

What would you like to add to make sure that I understand what has happened to your family?

Appendix B

CODING CATEGORIES

Category I: Becoming Homeless - The Story

Theme A: I Had No Choice, I Was Forced to Leave
Theme B: I Decided to Leave So We Could Have a Better Life
Theme C: We Tried to Avoid Homelessness by Staying with Relatives, But It Was Tense and Uncomfortable

Category II: Experiences in the Shelter System - Past

Theme A: It Was Traumatic To Live in the Hotels and Shelters
> Subtheme 1: We were living with a constant fear of danger
> Subtheme 2: I felt dehumanized and mistreated by the people in charge
> Subtheme 3: I felt isolated in the hotel
> Subtheme 4: Activities of daily living such as eating, sleeping, and bathing were stressful in the shelters and hotels

Theme B: I Liked the Shelters and Hotels Where We Stayed

Category III: Experiences in the Shelter System - Present

Theme A: I Feel Much More Secure Because I Know I Can Stay Here Until I Find an Apartment
> Subtheme 1: I wish I could stay here forever

Theme B: We Feel Safe Here
Theme C: We Have Almost Everything We Need Here

Theme D: I've Never Had So Many Opportunities In My Life
>Subtheme 1: The groups and meetings they have at this shelter are very helpful
>Subtheme 2: I feel my social worker cares about me and my family and helps us in many ways
>Subtheme 3: My social worker doesn't support me or respect my privacy
>Subtheme 4: The programs and activities for children at the shelter are good

Category IV: Emotional Consequences

Theme A: I Felt Anxious
Theme B: I Felt Depressed
>Subtheme 1: I felt hopeless
>Subtheme 2: I felt sad because I lost so much
>Subtheme 3: I'm ashamed to be homeless

Theme C: I Felt Angry
Theme D: My Health Suffered
Theme E: I Felt Relieved and Hopeful

Category V: Impact on Relationships

Theme A: Being Homeless Made it Difficult to Maintain Relationships
>Subtheme 1: I had to hide my relationship with the man with whom I'm involved

Theme B: Parenting In the Shelter Environment Has Been Challenging
>Subtheme 1: My child's behavior seemed to deteriorate after we became homeless
>Subtheme 2: I try to protect my children from the horror and danger associated with shelter life
>Subtheme 3: I feel guilty and inadequate as a parent for exposing my children to this

Theme C: It Was Difficult to Make New Friends

Category VI: Academic Consequences

Theme A: Homelessness Had a Negative Impact on My Children's Education

Theme B: I Hated Changing Schools So Often

Subtheme 1: I love the school I go to now and don't want to change again

Subtheme 2: I liked my old school better than this one and wish I could have stayed there

Subtheme 3: It seemed like I was always behind and trying to catch up with the rest of the class

Subtheme 4: Sometimes I was just too tired to pay attention to what was going on in school

Category VII: Supports

Theme A: My Family Is Supportive and Helpful

Subtheme 1: My child is a source of support and help

Subtheme 2: My mother is the most important person in the world to me

Subtheme 3: Relatives have helped us through this experience

Subtheme 4: I'm disappointed that my family has not been helpful or supportive enough

Theme B: Men Help Financially and Emotionally but They're Unreliable

Theme C: I Have Friends Who Help Me

Theme D: I'm Wary to Get Involved with the Other Residents

Category VIII: Coping Strategies

Theme A: I've Learned To Use the System To My Advantage

Subtheme 1: I've learned to be my own advocate

Subtheme 2: Entering the shelter system was my strategy for getting an apartment

Theme B: I Try to Avoid Problems By Staying Alone or With My Family

Theme C: Sometimes I Need a Drink to Calm Myself
Theme D: I Keep Busy So That I Don't Think About My
Situation Too Much
Theme E: I'm Always Ready To Defend My Integrity
Theme F: I Make New Friends As Quickly As I Can
Theme G: I Try To Follow the Rules So That We Don't
Get Thrown Out of Here on My Account
Theme H: My Belief in God Has Helped Me Through This
Theme I: I Found a Job To Help My Mother With
Expenses

Category IX: View of the Future

Theme A: I Want An Apartment That We Never Have To
Leave
Theme B: After We Move I Hope Our Problems Will
Disappear
Theme C: I Want to Work So I Can Get Off Welfare
        Subtheme 1: When I grow up I want to get a good
        job
Theme D: I'd Like To Live In A World Without
Homelessness

Index